MAKING SENSE OF
SCIENCE
AND
RELIGION

Strategies for the Classroom and Beyond

MAKING SENSE OF
SCIENCE
AND
RELIGION

Strategies for the Classroom and Beyond

Joseph W. Shane
Lee Meadows
Ronald S. Hermann
Ian C. Binns

National Science Teaching Association

Arlington, Virginia

National Science Teaching Association

Claire Reinburg, Director
Rachel Ledbetter, Managing Editor
Andrea Silen, Associate Editor
Jennifer Thompson, Associate Editor
Donna Yudkin, Book Acquisitions Manager

ART AND DESIGN
Will Thomas Jr., Director
Himabindu Bichali, Graphic Designer, cover and
    interior design

PRINTING AND PRODUCTION
Catherine Lorrain, Director

NATIONAL SCIENCE TEACHING ASSOCIATION
David L. Evans, Executive Director

1840 Wilson Blvd., Arlington, VA 22201
www.nsta.org/store
For customer service inquiries, please call 800-277-5300.

Library of Congress Cataloging-in-Publication Data
Names: Shane, Joseph W, 1969- author. | Meadows, Lee, author.
Title: Making sense of science and religion : strategies for the classroom and beyond / by Joseph W. Shane,
    Lee Meadows, Ronald S. Hermann, Ian C. Binns.
Description: Arlington, VA : National Science Teaching Association, [2020] | Includes bibliographical references
    and index. |
Identifiers: LCCN 2019022952 (print) | LCCN 2019022953 (ebook) | ISBN 9781681405766 (paperback) |
    ISBN 9781681405773 (pdf)
Subjects: LCSH: Religion and science.
Classification: LCC BL240.3 .S535 2019 (print) | LCC BL240.3 (ebook) | DDC 201/.65071073--dc23
LC record available at *https://lccn.loc.gov/2019022952*
LC ebook record available at *https://lccn.loc.gov/2019022953*

CONTENTS

Part I

Broadening Perspectives on Science-Religion Interactions

Part II

Practical Suggestions for All Teachers of Science

Part III

Beyond the Classroom

Preface

Dr. Shane, you are not taking this seriously ... and you need to.
—Preservice biology teacher, Shippensburg University, 2005

This class helped me to be less of a [jerk].
—Science-religion honors seminar student, Shippensburg University, 2015

For more than 10 years, understanding and addressing the complex interactions between science and religion has become part of my mission as a scientist, science teacher, and science teacher educator. I never intended to walk this path. Now, though, I embrace the role and I am grateful to a former student for, rather bluntly, initiating the interest that led me to this current effort to assist all teachers of science.

My first year at Shippensburg University in central Pennsylvania coincided with the 2005 *Kitzmiller v. Dover Area School District* trial (400 F. Supp. 2d 707, M.D. Pa.; see National Center for Science Education 2005), which is often referred to as Scopes II in reference to the well-known Scopes Monkey Trial from 1925 in Dayton, Tennessee. During the fall semester, a student in my science teaching methods class regularly came to my office hours to discuss the trial (the "this" in the first quote above). He was, to put it mildly, unimpressed with my knowledge of the proceedings, the legacy of the Scopes trial, other related Supreme Court cases, and evolutionary theory in general. He challenged me to take a more active role, and thus began my journey.

I first read Judge John E. Jones III's *Kitzmiller* ruling (National Center for Science Education 2005) where he determined the teaching of intelligent design to be inherently religious and thus in violation of the Constitution's Establishment Clause. After acquainting myself with the judicial history, I discovered vast areas of historical, philosophical, and theological scholarship devoted to nuanced understandings of science and religion that included, but also went beyond, specific scientific theories and concepts such as evolution, geochronology, climate, and genetics.

Since 2005, I have been fortunate to use these insights to better prepare my preservice science teachers. In 2007, the pastor at my church asked me to teach a three-week adult Sunday school class on science and religion, and I have been teaching similar courses ever since at regional Christian churches. I host an annual forum on science and religion at

Shippensburg, and the director of our honors program invited me to teach a seminar in 2015. The 12 students were, as far as I could tell, divided into three groups from a religious perspective. Four were active members of various Christian denominations, four had been active Christians earlier in their lives, and the remaining students were devoted atheists. An interesting group to be sure!

During one of the final class periods, a colleague with expertise on the sociology of science and religion (and author of the concluding chapter of this book) spoke to the class about his work, and he asked the students about their experiences in the course. One student quickly proclaimed, "This class helped me to be less of a [jerk]." She used a more college-appropriate and slightly cruder word, and I wish she had written this on the course evaluation.

My efforts eventually led me to engage my primary professional group, the Association for Science Teacher Education, a National Science Teaching Association affiliate. I befriended several colleagues who were addressing similar issues in their regions and science teacher preparation programs. After some conference presentations and a journal article, we decided that a broader effort was needed. And that's how this book was born. Those colleague friends are Lee, Ron, and Ian, the three other editors of this book.

With this book, we wish to assist you, our colleagues at all levels of science education, with understanding science-religion interactions in a broad sense to complement your personal experiences with your students and surrounding communities. We have written this book specifically for an audience of our fellow science educators, but it will also be of interest to any advocates for good science and quality science education, including parents, administrators, elected officials, and other policy makers. As you will notice from the modest chapter lengths and overall book size, it should be read as a primer that encourages additional reading and discussion. We asked each contributor to write in a conversational tone that is engaging to read while providing excellent resources for continued study and consideration.

We understand that science teachers have long seen the teaching of evolution in particular as a tough issue and an almost intractable one in many regions of the United States. To respond to this, we urge you to step beyond evolution into bigger issues at the interface of science and religion. We want to guide you in exploring those broader issues to provide a framework to make better sense of how to teach evolution and other science concepts. To genuinely understand science-religion relationships requires some understanding of history, sociology, religious experience and theology, and the Constitution and case law, as well as principles of good communication of complex ideas. You may even need to brush up on your own scientific knowledge. The other editors and I are not experts in all of these areas, so we have tapped the wisdom of a great group of additional authors to lend their perspectives.

Science has progressed to the point where it is rapidly changing our notions of matter, space, and time as well as addressing questions once thought to be outside of empirical investigation. Thus, it is no wonder we are challenged to reconcile scientific discoveries with our personal, often religious, beliefs. Sociobiology and neurology, for example, shed light on the fundamental aspects of human thought and behavior that can profoundly affect one's sense of identity and purpose. Physics, cosmology, and geology now contribute to our understanding of the origins of life. In this sense, science has grown far beyond isolated subdisciplines for the select few. Science is ingrained in our everyday culture, and it lends insight into and asks questions about topics of personal and universal significance, in a manner similar to literature, music, and other artistic expressions.

The chapter authors have demonstrated their ability to help navigate these waters. We invite you to do the same. We suggest that all teachers of science have some responsibility for understanding interactions between science and religion, two indisputably profound and durable cultural forces so often characterized as inherently in conflict with, or simply mutually exclusive of, one another. These all-too-familiar conflicting perspectives or simplistic dichotomies are inadequate in our view.

In Part I of the book, we introduce you to science-religion scholarship. We emphasize the historical roots and persistence of opposition to evolution given that it is the most prevalent science-religion theme in the United States. In addition to summarizing the relevant judicial and political history, we describe a precise framework for addressing science-religion issues in a legal, constitutional manner.

Part II is written for teachers of science at various levels: elementary/early childhood educators, middle school and high school science teachers, college professors and teacher educators, and colleagues who work in informal science education settings. We hope that you find this information useful not only for your work, but also for your collaborations with other science educators in your building, district, and beyond.

Part III recognizes that science-religion interactions often extend beyond our specific classrooms and other learning environments, and we offer advice for engaging other constituencies such as parents and families, administrators and school boards, legislators and policy makers, and faith communities. We include expert advice about how to best respond when issues of science and religion arise, and we look to the future regarding how controversies around teaching evolution might shift in the years ahead.

We have invited authors who are in many ways personally and professionally invested in these ideas. Some contributors are K–12 teachers and university professors. Some are science teacher educators like us. Others are from prominent organizations such as the American Association for the Advancement of Science and the Smithsonian National Museum of Natural History. We have encouraged them all to share memorable and illustrative stories along with their expertise, selected references that are most appropriate for all teachers of science, and take-home advice and recommendations for action. We are hopeful that you will find the concise yet comprehensive nature of this book useful to your everyday work and to your greater understanding of science and religion.

Dr. Joseph W. Shane
Shippensburg University of Pennsylvania

REFERENCE

National Center for Science Education. 2005. *Kitzmiller v. Dover*: Intelligent design on trial. *https://ncse.com/library-resource/kitzmiller-v-dover-intelligent-design-trial.*

About the Authors and Contributors

AUTHORS

Joseph W. Shane, **professor of chemistry and science education, Shippensburg University (Shippensburg, PA).** As professor of chemistry and science education at Shippensburg University, Joe has responsibilities both to the chemistry department and to the programs, both undergraduate and graduate, that license preservice secondary (7–12) science teachers. In addition to teaching a variety of chemistry courses, he teaches pedagogical methods in science, supervises secondary science teachers, teaches an honors seminar, and conducts outreach on the intersections of science and religion.

Lee Meadows, **professor of science education, University of Alabama at Birmingham (Birmingham, AL).** Lee is a professor of science education at the University of Alabama at Birmingham. A teacher at heart, he has taught high school chemistry, physics, and physical science as well as college chemistry, general teaching methods, and science methods. Throughout his career, Lee has written and spoken on the teaching of evolution in the American South, and he is the author of *The Missing Link: An Inquiry Approach for Teaching All Students About Evolution.*

Ronald S. Hermann, **professor of science education, Towson University (Towson, MD).** Ron is the author of several peer-reviewed articles that explore the teaching and learning of evolution. He has conducted more than 20 presentations on the topic of evolution education and is the recipient of the Association for Science Teacher Education 2018 Award for Outstanding Science Teacher Educator of the Year in recognition of his work. Ron is a science educator at Towson University where he works to prepare preservice K–12 teachers of science.

 *Ian C. Binns,* **associate professor of science education, University of North Carolina at Charlotte (Charlotte, NC).** As an associate professor of elementary science education at the University of North Carolina at Charlotte, Ian does research that primarily focuses on the interaction between science and religion. His goal is to help facilitate understanding of science and religion, what makes them each unique, their interaction, and how they both benefit society. Specifically, Ian's research looks at how preservice elementary teachers' scientific literacy and faith-based beliefs influence their perceptions of how socioscientific issues—such as evolution, creationism, and intelligent design—should be addressed in the classroom.

CONTRIBUTORS

Curtis L. Baxter III, **senior program associate, American Association for the Advancement of Science (Washington, DC).** Curtis is a senior program associate working primarily on the Science for Seminaries project of the American Association for the Advancement of Science's Dialogue on Science, Ethics, and Religion program. The project aids seminaries in integrating forefront science into their core curriculum. After finishing his BA in religious studies with a minor in biochemistry, Curtis earned a master of theological studies degree from Wesley Theological Seminary, where he focused on ethics and historical/ public theology.

Mark Bloom, **professor of biology and science education, Dallas Baptist University (Dallas, TX).** Mark teaches biology and science pedagogy at Dallas Baptist University (DBU). He holds a BS in biology from DBU (1994), an MS in biology from Baylor University (1997), and a PhD in science education from Texas Christian University (2008). His primary research interests center on the philosophy of science, the intersection of science and religion, and the public's understanding of religiously sensitive, sociocultural biological issues.

Lisa Borgerding, **associate professor of science education, Kent State University (Kent, OH).** As an associate professor of science education at Kent State University, Lisa teaches undergraduate-, master's-, and doctoral-level courses in science education and research methodology. Her research centers on the teaching and learning of biological evolution from early childhood through college, the nature of science instruction, preservice and inservice teacher development, and service learning in teacher education.

Jennifer Collins, **manager of ocean education, Smithsonian National Museum of Natural History (Washington, DC).** Jennifer has spent her career in science education, both as a middle and high school science teacher and as an informal educator. She has contributed to the development of resources such as "Understanding Evolution" (*https://evolution.berkeley.edu*) and "Understanding Science" (*https://undsci.berkeley.edu*), facilitated countless professional development programs (including ones out at sea!), and worked with amazing scientists and educators to inspire scientific understanding and an appreciation for a wide range of audiences.

Christine DiPasquale, **senior program associate, American Association for the Advancement of Science (Washington, DC).** Christine is a senior program associate for the American Association for the Advancement of Science's Dialogue on Science, Ethics, and Religion program, and she administered the Bringing Forefront Science to Religion Reporters project. An award-winning journalist, Christine has specialized in reporting on intersections of religion and public life for a variety of national and local media outlets, including *The Huffington Post, Jersey Shore Patch, Slate, Christianity Today, Urban Faith, The High Calling,* and *On Faith.* She graduated summa cum laude in journalism and media studies from the Rutgers University School of Communication and Information.

Nathan Einsig, **science teacher, Mechanicsburg Area Senior High School (Mechanicsburg, PA).** Nathan, a science educator at Mechanicsburg Area Senior High, began his teaching career 13 years ago after working in the private science industry as a software engineer focused on systems used for scientific research. His responsibilities at Mechanicsburg have included chairing the science department, teaching ninth-grade Earth and space science, and offering an advanced geoscience elective to seniors. Nathan holds a BS in computer science from James Madison University, a post-baccalaureate certificate in Earth science and education from West Chester University, and an MS in geoscience from Mississippi State University. He has presented at conferences on topics such as the intersection of science and religion in the public school system and teaching climate science with fidelity.

Barbara Forrest, **professor of philosophy (retired), Southeastern Louisiana University (Holden, LA).** Barbara taught philosophy for 37 years prior to retirement. She devoted her professional career as a philosopher to scholarship about the issues of creationism and the separation of church and state. She also served on the Board of Directors of the National Center for Science Education and Americans United for Separation of Church and State. She has been a pro-science activist at the national level as well as in her home state of Louisiana.

Josh Hubbard, **science teacher, Inter-City Baptist School (Allen Park, MI).** Josh is a biology teacher with 12 years of experience. He has taught life science, biology, and a senior biology elective, and he holds a master's degree in science education from Wayne State University. Josh also consults for a project-based inquiry science curriculum, where he provides professional development for teachers looking to shift the way they teach science.

Se Kim, **deputy chief programs officer, American Association for the Advancement of Science (Washington, DC).** Se is the deputy chief programs officer responsible for aligning the strategic goals and outcomes of all the science society and policy programs at the association. Previously serving as the associate director of the Dialogue on Science, Ethics, and Religion program, she has a deep commitment to bridging scientific and religious communities through constructive dialogue and education. After Se received a PhD in molecular and human genetics from the Baylor College of Medicine, she continued her research at Rice University as a National Institutes of Health's National Research Service Award postdoctoral fellow. She holds an MBA from the Robert H. Smith School of Business at the University of Maryland and has an interest in implementing initiatives and mobilizing stakeholders for mission-based organizations.

David Long, **assistant professor of STEM education, Morehead State University (Morehead, KY).** David's research examines the cognitive, social, and philosophical dimensions of student and teacher understanding of evolution, climate change science, and genetic engineering, with an emphasis on how political and religious ideology mediates science education implementation in schools, universities, and the civic discourse. He is currently an assistant professor of STEM education at Morehead State University.

Trish Mace, **director, University of Oregon's Charleston Marine Life Center (Charleston, OR).** Trish is the director of the University of Oregon's Charleston Marine Life Center and previously was the manager of ocean education and partnerships at the Smithsonian's National Museum of Natural History. She has served on the Federal Interagency Working Group on Ocean Education and on the Centers for Ocean Sciences Education Excellence council. Trish has worked with a number of schools and nonprofit organizations on various ocean education projects, both domestically and internationally. Her interests span the fields of science communication and education in both informal and formal settings, with a focus on ocean and climate science.

Kathleen (Casey) Oberlin, **assistant professor, Grinnell College (Grinnell, IA).** Casey, an assistant professor of sociology at Grinnell College, completed her PhD in sociology at Indiana University. She is currently completing a manuscript based on over three years of fieldwork at the Creation Museum in Kentucky built by Answers in Genesis, an organization tied to the broader Young Earth Creationist movement. This work received funding from the National Science Foundation and the Social Science Research Council, among others.

Robert O'Malley, **project director, American Association for the Advancement of Science (Washington, DC).** Rob is the project director in the Dialogue on Science, Ethics, and Religion program at the American Association for the Advancement of Science. He holds a

BA in anthropology and zoology from Miami University of Ohio, an MA in anthropology from the University of Alberta, and a PhD in integrative and evolutionary biology from the University of Southern California. Rob has led or participated in research projects on a diversity of nonhuman primates both in captivity and in the wild, to better understand primate behavioral ecology as well as to inform scientific perspectives and hypotheses regarding human origins and evolution. He has taught biological anthropology courses at Kenyon College, the George Washington University, and the University of Maryland, and he regularly participates in public science engagement activities.

Briana Pobiner, **human origins scientist and educator, Smithsonian National Museum of Natural History (Washington, DC).** Briana is a paleoanthropologist who also leads the education and outreach efforts of the Smithsonian's Human Origins Program. In addition to her scientific research on human evolution, which focuses on early human diet, she manages public programs, website content, social media, and exhibition volunteer training. Briana most recently developed a research program in evolution education and science communication, and she strives to effectively communicate about evolution and climate science with a variety of audiences.

Lindsey Porter, **science teacher, Mechanicsburg Area Senior High School (Mechanicsburg, PA).** Lindsey has been teaching biology and Earth and space science at Mechanicsburg Area Senior High since 2009, after transitioning from the human services field. Her background includes a BS in biology from Messiah College, an MS in the science of instruction from Drexel University, and an MS in geoscience from Mississippi State University. Lindsey extends her teaching to the community, collaborating on talks and panels about issues connecting science and society.

Jennifer J. Wiseman, **program director, American Association for the Advancement of Science (Washington, DC).** Jennifer is the program director of the American Association for the Advancement of Science's Dialogue on Science, Ethics, and Religion program as well as an astrophysicist at NASA, where she is the senior project scientist for the Hubble Space Telescope. She studies the formation of stars and planetary systems using radio, optical, and infrared telescopes. Jennifer studied physics for her bachelor's degree at the Massachusetts Institute of Technology, discovering comet Wiseman-Skiff in 1987. After earning her PhD in astronomy from Harvard University in 1995, she continued her research as a Jansky Fellow at the National Radio Astronomy Observatory, as a Hubble Fellow at Johns Hopkins University. Jennifer also has an interest in national science policy and has served as an American Physical Society Congressional Science Fellow on Capitol Hill. She enjoys giving talks on the excitement of science and astronomy to schools, youth and church groups, and civic organizations. She is a councilor of the American Astronomical Society and a former president of the American Scientific Affiliation.

OTHER INPUT

The following individuals also provided valuable input:

- *Mark Dalrymple,* Dialogue on Science, Ethics, and Religion program intern, American Association for the Advancement of Science (Washington, DC)

- *Robert Eshbach,* science teacher, Dover Area High School (Dover, PA)

- *Jennifer Miller,* science teacher, Dover Area High School (Dover, PA)

- *Kenneth Miller,* professor of biology, Brown University (Providence, RI)

- *Eric Rothschild,* former senior litigation counsel, Americans United for Separation of Church and State (Washington, DC)

PART I

Broadening Perspectives on
Science-Religion Interactions

Science and Religion as Part of Our Professional Responsibilities

Joseph W. Shane, Lee Meadows, Ronald S. Hermann, and Ian C. Binns

Teaching is often more about establishing and building trust with our students and less about the conventional content and practices of biology, chemistry, Earth and space sciences, environmental science, and physics. Simply put, when there is mutual trust and respect in a classroom, enduring learning occurs. This is obvious to say, difficult to achieve, and marvelous when it happens!

Like many people, our students will sometimes come to us with religiously based understandings of the natural world and their roles in it. Other students may be antagonistic toward these perspectives. Others still will wonder what all the fuss is about and would just as soon stick to the science. As usual, our job is to convey and model science in the midst of all of our students' complex preconceptions, misconceptions, beliefs, values, joys, and social anxieties.

We believe interactions between science and religion are an inevitable part of teaching science in 21st-century America. As all good teachers do, we've learned to thoughtfully anticipate, and respond to, our students' prior knowledge and beliefs regardless of their origins or our personal perspectives. We do not, however, expect this to be easy, and the authors in this book will make their separate cases as to why you should care and what specifically you can do to, quoting a good friend that you will meet in Chapter 7, "bring the threat level down" when religion is brought up.

In this first chapter, we make the argument that addressing science and religion is, in fact, part of our collective job. We review four domains of science teaching to make our case, and to assist you in explaining, justifying, and defending your choices to your students, colleagues, and community. In our view, science-religion interactions are perfectly consistent with the well-known nature of science (NOS) literature, with professional standards, with general ethical principles and responsibilities of all teachers, and with scientific inquiry. Science educators at all levels have the potential to "move the needle" on how students understand similarities and differences between scientific and religious worldviews. We also have the professional responsibility for doing just that.

DISTINGUISHING SCIENCE AND RELIGION
VIA THE NATURE OF SCIENCE

Before reviewing the various aspects of NOS, we need to ask a broader question—namely, what is science? As science teachers you may not ask yourself this question very often. But it is important because this understanding is a key part of addressing science-religion interactions, and basic misunderstandings about NOS are often central to the distrust in science and scientists that is expressed by people of faith.

One particularly concise definition states that science is "the use of evidence to construct testable explanations and predictions of natural phenomena, as well as the knowledge generated through this process" (National Academy of Sciences and Institute of Medicine 2008, p. 10). This definition includes key characteristics that distinguish science from other ways of knowing: empirical evidence, testable explanations and predictions, and natural phenomena. An additional characteristic is that science involves a scientific community. This reinforces the notion that scientific research is ultimately collaborative, reproducible, and subject to expert peer review. Each of these characteristics is an essential part of the development and acceptance of scientific knowledge.

With this general understanding, let's move to NOS, which is in essence "the epistemology of science, science as a way of knowing, or the values and beliefs inherent to scientific knowledge and its development" (Lederman 2007, p. 833). While there are many lists outlining aspects of NOS, the following characteristics are commonly cited:

- *Science requires empirical evidence.* This one is straightforward. In order for something to be accepted as scientific, there must be evidence based on observable, verifiable data. No scientific explanations are considered without empirical evidence. It is important to note that empirical evidence can be both quantitative and qualitative descriptions of the natural world.

- *Science is tentative.* Scientific knowledge is not absolute, meaning it is subject to change. This happens when either new evidence is discovered or new ways are discovered to evaluate existing evidence. This process may not always be quick, but over time when new instrumentation or new evidence comes to light, scientific explanations can, and will, change.

- *Science is subjective.* This suggests that scientists' backgrounds influence what they investigate, what they observe, and how they interpret evidence. To be a detached observer in a purely objective sense is simply not possible, even though many people think that is how science works.

- *Science is creative.* Scientists use creativity and imagination throughout the scientific process. This includes developing research questions, designing investigations, and formulating explanations of their findings.

- *Science is influenced by social and cultural values.* What scientists and scientific communities value guides questions that scientists ask, influences ways scientists conduct research, and potentially advances or impedes scientific progress.

- *Scientific knowledge comes from both observations and inferences.* "Seeing is believing" is a common idiom and implies that if you cannot directly see something, then it is not real. In reality, however, scientists cannot artificially separate observations from their inferred explanations and provisional hypotheses.

- *Scientific theories and laws are distinct, but equally important, aspects of science.* Theories are not merely hunches or guesses, but rather they are the overarching frameworks based on overwhelming evidence that guide inquiry within a scientific discipline. Theories explain and predict observed phenomena. Laws, on the other hand, are the most basic descriptions of observed phenomena that apply across all disciplines. In science, theories do not grow up and become laws. Atomic *theory* and the *law* of conservation of energy (i.e., the first law of thermodynamics) are straightforward examples.

Ultimately, NOS makes it a quintessentially human endeavor, and this is what makes science so fascinating, especially when compared to other domains where the human dimension is perhaps more obviously central like economics, politics, and, yes, religion. Individual scientists bring a finite amount of knowledge and cultural experience to bear in order to explain evidence derived from experiments, observations of nature, and artifacts from the past. Provisional hypotheses are creative, subjective assertions that are typically consistent with the currently accepted theoretical framework. Hypotheses must be tested against further evidence. Inquiries must be repeated and subjected to review by qualified experts via peer-reviewed publications and conference presentations.

If sufficient evidence accumulates within the global scientific community, previously accepted ideas are discarded, often reluctantly. On occasion, entire underlying theoretical frameworks are altered so as to change how we perceive the natural world. These internal checks and balances are imperfect to be sure (plenty of examples of fraud exist), but the success and impact of the collective, global scientific endeavor are undeniable and unmatched.

In our view, this basic understanding of science goes a long way toward addressing misunderstandings that the public frequently has about science. The common dismissive statement that evolution is "just a theory" falls flat, as does the claim that scientists are "biased." The inherently tentative nature of science is not a weakness, but rather a self-correcting historical reality and a strength of science that separates it from other ways of knowing about the world. Scientists rarely speak with absolute certainty, but this is not evidence of anxious doubt or irreconcilable gaps in scientific knowledge. The measured tones of science merely suggest that there is always more to know.

SCIENCE-RELIGION THEMES IN PROFESSIONAL STANDARDS

It probably comes as no surprise that the word *religion* or any derivations do not appear directly within any science education standards insofar as we can tell. There are no explicit statements, suggested lessons, or assessments that teachers can reference to teach students about science-religion interactions. Quite frankly, if such guidance were already available in our professional standards, this book would not be necessary.

Upon closer examination, however, science-religion themes can easily be gleaned from science standards at all levels. In particular, national and state standards unequivocally provide support for NOS instruction, the use of historical case studies, and attending to students' prior beliefs and, in so doing, justify the responsible inclusion of religion for strictly educational purposes.

Veteran science educators might recall the beginnings of the "science for all" movement with the publication of *Science for All Americans* (*SFAA*) by the American Association for the Advancement of Science (AAAS; 1990) and the follow-up document used to write standards and curricula, *Benchmarks for Science Literacy* (AAAS 19933). Entire chapters are devoted to NOS instruction, and the following statement from *SFAA* recognizes the limits of scientific inquiry in addressing what are often religiously based issues for our students:

> *There are many matters that cannot usefully be examined in a scientific way. There are, for instance, beliefs that—by their very nature—cannot be proved or disproved (such as the existence of supernatural powers and beings, or the true purposes of life). In other cases, a scientific approach that may be valid is likely to be rejected as irrelevant by people who hold to certain beliefs (such as in miracles, fortune-telling, astrology, and superstition). Nor do scientists have the means to settle issues concerning good and evil, although they can sometimes contribute to the discussion of such issues by identifying the likely consequences of particular actions, which may be helpful in weighing alternatives.* (AAAS 1990, p. 100)

You may be interested to know that AAAS has an ongoing initiative to help scientists better communicate with religious individuals and institutions. Leaders from the AAAS Dialogue on Science, Ethics, and Religion program give us their insights and advice in Chapter 11.

Published shortly after *Benchmarks*, the *National Science Education Standards* (*NSES*; National Research Council [NRC] 1996) maintained strong support for NOS instruction, and these national documents formed the basis for state and local standards and curricula for a generation. Today, we are familiar with the *Next Generation Science Standards* (*NGSS*; NGSS Lead States 2013) and its *SFAA* analogue, *A Framework for K–12 Science Education* (NRC 2012). While NOS instruction is not featured as prominently in the *NGSS*, following public input it was emphasized to a greater degree, primarily in Appendix H of the *NGSS*. Appendix H, easily found online, addresses NOS directly and offers an extensive rubric for the NOS understandings that children should develop at different grade levels. Broad statements about NOS made in this appendix and in *A Framework for K–12 Science Education* are quite consistent with previous documents used to write state and local science education standards.

Additionally, national standards have consistently supported using historical case studies to teach science. The *NGSS*, like its antecedents, recommends student understanding of the Copernican revolution, Newtonian mechanics, Lyell's study of rocks and fossils, Darwin's theory of biological evolution, and Watson and Crick's molecular model of genetics. In each of these and many more examples, the implications for religious and other social perspectives are profound. Consider this excerpt from *SFAA*:

> *The science of Newton was so successful that its influence spread far beyond physics and astronomy. Physical principles and Newton's mathematical way of deriving consequences from them together became the model for all other sciences. The belief grew that eventually all of nature could be explained in terms of physics and mathematics and that nature therefore could run by itself, without the help or attention of gods—although Newton himself saw his physics as demonstrating the hand of God acting on the universe. Social thinkers considered whether governments could be designed like a Newtonian solar system, with a balance of forces and actions that would ensure regular operation and long-term stability.* (AAAS 1990, p. 113)

Other scientists—Copernicus, Galileo, Darwin—and their discoveries also had widespread cultural influence on domains such as economics, government, and religion. We recommend that such historical examples be used alongside more contemporary science such as Big Bang cosmology, genetic engineering, climate science, and discoveries of fundamental forces and particles. The focus, of course, should always be on the core scientific principles.

Finally, and perhaps most importantly, we teach the students we have and build upon their prior knowledge, beliefs, and experiences. This is the central tenet of constructivist teaching. To this end, we found the following excerpt from *SFAA* particularly powerful:

> *But effective learning often requires more than just making multiple connections of new ideas to old ones; it sometimes requires that people restructure their thinking radically. That is, to incorporate some new idea, learners must change the connections among the things they already know, or even discard some long-held beliefs about the world. The alternatives to the necessary restructuring are to distort the new information to fit their old ideas or to reject the new information entirely. Students come to school with their own ideas, some correct and some not, about almost every topic they are likely to encounter. If their intuition and misconceptions are ignored or dismissed out of*

hand, their original beliefs are likely to win out in the long run, even though they may give the test answers their teachers want. Mere contradiction is not sufficient; students must be encouraged to develop new views by seeing how such views help them make better sense of the world. (AAAS 1990, p. 145)

Aspects of this statement can be found in almost any set of academic standards, but none of us needs standards-based justification for transforming students' understanding of science in a manner that respects who they are when they walk into our classrooms, labs, museums, and environmental education centers. If some of their knowledge and beliefs about the natural world are influenced by their religious upbringing, so be it. We are obliged to account for this, and we assert by counterpoint that to ignore relationships between science and religion is irresponsible from historical and pedagogical perspectives.

SCIENCE-RELIGION INTERACTIONS AS AN ETHICAL RESPONSIBILITY

As science teachers, we have a professional responsibility to help students learn, and come to appreciate, science as a human endeavor. That responsibility entails, among other things, teaching scientific concepts that are considered valid as well as the broad nature and practices of science. There are numerous ways to approach the interaction between science and religion but presenting the two ways of knowing as being in conflict is not a complete representation. Moving away from the idea that science and religion are necessarily in conflict, by either their methods or underlying assumptions, is a theme repeated throughout this book. We have an ethical responsibility to help students learn science without feeling that their religious beliefs are being challenged or contradicted by us or their peers. Students may have questions about the interaction between science and religion, but no student in a public-school classroom should feel as though he or she needs to choose between science and faith. Moreover, by maintaining a civil dialogue, we can help ensure that all students feel safe expressing their views.

Make no mistake, we are science teachers and our primary responsibilities are to teach science content and skills. However, we have a choice of the type of experiences we provide to help students learn science and to understand differences between science and other ways of knowing about the world, like religion.

Defining what science is can be difficult at times and there are certainly fringe areas that challenge our understanding of the differences between science and religion. Much like the thought experiment where we ask our students to define a game, at first glance this seems easy, but once we begin the task we find it is far more difficult than we anticipated. We must develop a definition that includes all things that are games and excludes all things that are not games. Games, as most employ the term, can include a wide array of individual and multiplayer activities that may be mental, physical, or both. It is usually not too hard to develop a counterexample of something that is not considered a game to identify a logical flaw. Not many people consider taking a science class or conducting a scientific inquiry to be a game, but both certainly share some traits. The point of such a mental exercise is not to suggest that there are no differences between science and religion, but to acknowledge and demonstrate to students that there are different ways of making sense of the world. Our responsibility is to consider the interactions between science and religion and to extend students' thinking beyond a singular model based on inevitable conflict. Moreover, we ask that they understand science regardless of their religious beliefs.

> *"We have an ethical responsibility to help students learn science without feeling that their religious beliefs are being challenged or contradicted by us or their peers."*

Consider how, in situations where students in our science classes struggle because of a lack of mathematics or writing skills, we take time to help them in those areas. We suggest that all of us have an obligation to do so with science-religion interactions as well. Just as with lessons that review graphing, fractions, or basic syntax, consider doing something similar when the topic addresses an interaction between science and religion. Spending a little class time can pay dividends later when students who may have been initially resistant become more receptive.

But why should *you* be the one to address science and religion issues? Simple. Ask yourself the following question: If you don't teach students about the interaction between science and other ways of knowing about the world, who will? It is not reasonable to assume that your colleagues who teach the grade band or subject before or after you will do so. There is also no guarantee that if they do that, they will address it in a meaningful way that creates enduring understanding. These are difficult topics to address and many students (like people in general) possess views that are resistant to change. When students enter a science classroom, for example, and spout the phrase "it's just a theory" when discussing topics such as evolution or Big Bang cosmology, it may be a pretty good indication that the student has not had the opportunity, in a nonthreatening environment, to understand the powerful status that theories hold in the sciences. This phrase may also show that they have not developed a sophisticated understanding of what makes science different from other ways of knowing. Science teachers can help students sort out and discern the precise meanings of words such as *belief*, *knowledge*, and *evidence* as they are used in scientific and religious contexts. Without such understanding, how can we fault students for not accepting evolution and other topics that, for many, challenge strongly held religious beliefs?

In our view, every type of science educator has an ethical obligation to minimize the perceived conflict between science and religion. When students hear a consistent message during science instruction—that they can learn science while maintaining their religious beliefs—they are much more willing to learn regardless of messages to the contrary that they might hear outside of your classroom.

APPROACHING SCIENCE-RELIGION RELATIONSHIPS VIA INQUIRY

At this point, you could easily be wondering, "OK, but how can I do all of that?" The task of helping students make sense of science-religion interactions probably seems difficult to many of you. Furthermore, those of you who have students who resist learning about evolution, especially those who do so because of their religious beliefs, know firsthand how difficult it can be to navigate the interactions of science and religion in your classrooms. Discussions can easily blow up into big conflicts! Thankfully, though, the shift in American science teaching toward inquiry-based approaches helps us significantly.

You're probably familiar with inquiry, and we offer more specific examples in Part II of this book. Calls for its use began in the 1990s, especially when the *NSES* focused America's science teachers on inquiry as the pedagogy best suited for developing scientific literacy. You're probably also familiar with how the *NGSS* have broadened the call to inquiry by implementing eight science and engineering practices (SEPs). No longer can American science teachers stand at the front of the classroom and just talk science to students. Now, we need to engage our students in the practices of science and engineering so that the students make sense of scientific explanations based on their examination of evidence.

Teaching via inquiry and with the SEPs creates for students a cycle of evidence and explanation. Students begin the cycle by asking questions, defining problems, or carrying out investigations. Because some evidence is difficult or dangerous to collect, students cannot do hands-on science all the time. Sometimes they need to be given evidence to examine. They then begin to examine the evidence through practices such as developing models, analyzing data, and using computational thinking. They are now in the minds-on part of science where they are starting to make sense of the evidence they saw earlier. We then guide them into the explanation phase of the cycle where they begin formally constructing explanations, arguing from evidence, and developing ways to communicate their newly constructed ideas. As with all of science, these new explanations generate new questions and the cycle begins again with students seeking new evidence for these new questions.

This immersion in evidence and explanation provided by inquiry and the SEPs allows teachers to build a classroom climate in which positive dialogue about the interactions of science and religion can occur. As students move through the cycle again and again, they begin to realize that what counts as scientific evidence is data collected from the natural world. Humans pay attention to many things other than scientific evidence as they make sense of the world, but only data collected through scientific practices counts as scientific evidence. Similarly, as students have multiple experiences creating scientific explanations, they begin to realize that science restricts itself to explanations provided by natural laws.

Humans often use supernatural explanations, but students understand that science has to stay neutral about the supernatural, arguing neither for nor against it. These understandings, rooted in NOS, are ones we can guide students to solidify for themselves when they experience them through multiple cycles of inquiry.

When immersion in evidence and explanations guides students to solid understandings of what science is, and what it is not, they are ready to see how science and religion can interact with one another without having to be either totally right or totally wrong. Imagine teaching a high school biology class and spending the first two-thirds of the year grounding all that students learn in evidence and helping them realize what counts as good scientific evidence as you teach such topics as photosynthesis, ecosystems, and genetics. Now, if you continue that focus on evidence as you begin the evolution unit, students are less apt to cry foul that you are teaching offensive content. Instead, you can make clear that they are going to be looking first at actual evidence for evolution, basing all of their learning in real data, and then working together to see how scientists explain that evidence limiting themselves to natural processes. They may dislike the evidence or even refuse to accept the scientific explanations, but they will have a better understanding of why evolution counts as science. This is because when students have consistent experiences developing explanations in a classroom implementing SEPs, they begin to develop a trust regarding how scientific explanations are developed. These experiences eventually prepare students with the ability to contrast scientific ways of knowing the world with other ways, including religion, because they are developing solid understandings of science itself. This is especially important for students who resist learning about evolution because of misconceptions they hold about how science works. (See Chapter 7 for more recommendations for middle school and high school teachers.)

Inquiry and the SEPs also can cause another key shift in the classroom allowing students, including those resistant to evolution, to engage in learning about the interactions of science and religion. With these approaches, we move the culture of our classrooms from an authoritarian approach in which we might be seen by some of our students as preaching about science to a more democratic approach in which multiple perspectives are allowed. In this culture, positive dialogue about science and religion can even thrive. The more democratic approach of the SEPs creates a classroom rich in student dialogue around "What evidence do you see?" and "How do you explain this?" Because students and their teachers are working together to understand the science, students are more free to express their thoughts and beliefs about the interactions they see between science and religion and receive guidance from their teacher.

MOVING FORWARD

It is not an exaggeration to state that, in order to responsibly address science and religion in the 21st century, we need you. Each of us has a role in helping our students, colleagues, and communities move beyond what might often seem like warring factions or irreconcilable viewpoints. With our collective backgrounds and experiences in science and pedagogy, who is better positioned to take up this necessary challenge?

We hope that this first chapter—part literature review and part editorial—provides you with sufficient professional justification and encourages action. If you need broader historical, cultural, and/or sociological perspectives, or if you are concerned about the legal ramifications of your actions, then read on in Part I. If you want specific ideas for teaching in your particular context offered by like-minded colleagues, we encourage you to skip ahead to the relevant chapters in Part II. If you want to consider science-religion perspectives that go beyond specific classroom issues, then Part III might be your next stop. This chapter is just the beginning.

REFERENCES

American Association for the Advancement of Science (AAAS). 1990. *Science for all Americans*. New York: Oxford University Press.

American Association for the Advancement of Science (AAAS). 1993. *Benchmarks for science literacy*. New York: Oxford University Press.

Lederman, N. G. 2007. Nature of science: Past, present, and future. In *Handbook of research on science education*, ed. S. K. Abell and N. Lederman, 831. Mahwah, NJ: Lawrence Erlbaum Associates.

National Academy of Sciences and Institute of Medicine. 2008. *Science, evolution, and creationism*. Washington, DC: National Academies Press.

National Research Council (NRC). 1996. *National Science Education Standards*. Washington, DC: National Academies Press.

National Research Council (NRC). 2012. *A framework for K–12 science education: Practices, crosscutting concepts, and core ideas*. Washington, DC: National Academies Press.

NGSS Lead States. 2013. *Next Generation Science Standards: For states, by states*. Washington, DC: National Academies Press. *www.nextgenscience.org/next-generation-science-standards*.

The Need for History and Evolution as a Science-Religion Case Study

Joseph W. Shane

In the preface, I noted how my interest in science and religion began in 2005 with the *Kitzmiller v. Dover Area School District* trial (National Center for Science Education 2005; Wikipedia contributors 2019). To be honest, I did not view this as an opportunity for any kind of scholarly work. I was, admittedly, shocked and frustrated after the trial and after reading Judge Jones's (2005) compelling decision. I was angry at the two school board members who pressured Dover High School's science teachers to include intelligent design as an alternative to evolution. I could not understand why an organization like the Discovery Institute's Center for Science and Culture and fellow chemist Michael Behe from Lehigh University would file amicus briefs and offer supporting courtroom testimony. None of this made any sense to me at the time as either a career-long science educator or a practicing Christian.

Outrage, however, was not a useful long-term strategy. My perspective changed dramatically when I began to read about the history of science and religion and eventually teach it to audiences such as my preservice science teachers, students in my university's honors program (Shane 2019), and congregations from my Presbyterian denomination. As I quickly discovered, there is a vast body of literature that explores these issues from every imaginable angle. I have selected a few key resources to help you shed light and disperse a lot of unnecessary heat in the vital and ongoing science-religion dialogue.

I begin by introducing Ian Barbour, who is generally credited with establishing science-religion interactions as a historical discipline. He provides us with a clear set of categories that serves as a useful starting point for discussing science and religion with students of all ages. Knowing that we can learn from the past but live in the present, I provide a few historical and contemporary examples, many of which are from my own experiences. Next, I transition to what is, not surprisingly, *the* science-religion issue in contemporary society, namely the historical origins of, and ongoing opposition to, teaching evolution. As we will see, this is largely a modern, American, and narrowly Christian phenomenon that remains a prominent feature of our cultural and educational landscape more than 150 years after the publication of Darwin's (1859) *On the Origin of Species*. As with many chapters in this book, I conclude with some general advice for all teachers of science and offer suggestions for further reading and concrete actions you can take.

UNDERSTANDING SCIENCE-RELIGION RELATIONSHIPS: THE LEGACY OF IAN BARBOUR

We are indebted to Barbour for giving us a platform for viewing science and religion together. Given his background as a physicist and formal training in theology, he epitomizes what sociologist of religion Ecklund (2010) asserts are sorely needed today: namely, boundary pioneers who can responsibly and courageously address science-religion interactions.

Here I reference Barbour's (1997) seminal text, *Religion and Science: Historical and Contemporary Issues*, that compares science and religion with respect to their founding ideas and practices, charts general interactions between science and religion through and since the 17th and 18th centuries, and describes the varied theological responses to advances in physics, astronomy, and biology. Barbour acknowledged that his work focused primarily on Christianity-and-science relationships in Western culture. It is beyond the scope of this chapter, as well as my personal breadth of knowledge, to give a more religiously pluralistic treatment. However, some of the resources cited later do discuss science-religion relationships from other perspectives: Judaism, Islam, Hinduism, Buddhism, atheism, indigenous religions, and more. I encourage you to adapt these additional resources as needed to your students and communities.

Barbour does not provide simple dictionary definitions of either science or religion before making comparisons. There is, however, significant overlap between his descriptions of scientific inquiry and the nature of science (NOS) that we discussed in Chapter 1. If you need a refresher, feel free to circle back to that chapter.

In characterizing religious belief, Barbour notes several consistencies with science. In particular, he suggests that interpretations of religious experiences require individual creativity and explanation using concepts that are often analogies. In this sense, religion is similar to the theory-laden, observational nature of science. Religious adherents' experiences of an omnipresent creator, personal transformations, understanding of suffering, or moral obligation are always viewed through the lens of their prior experiences and beliefs as well as their faith communities' accepted stories and rituals derived from sacred texts and oral traditions. Experience, story, and ritual are the data of religion according to Barbour, although these data are not empirically testable and generalizable in the same manner as science.

A more practical concern for teachers is how science-religion relationships have been viewed throughout history. To this end, Barbour introduced a four-part framework: (1) the warfare or conflict thesis, (2) the independence approach, (3) integration, and (4) dialogue.

Warfare or Conflict

The first approach is familiar to us given the circumstances in which science teachers are often directly involved. The warfare or conflict position suggests that science and religion are philosophically and/or methodologically opposed and that progress in one field necessarily impedes the other. One advocate for this position was John William Draper, a chemistry professor at Hampden-Sydney College in Virginia and the first president of the American Chemical Society. Draper (1876) accepted Enlightenment philosopher August Comte's prediction—a periodic claim made to this day—that society would eventually progress away from religion in favor of a more evidence- and reason-based society. In our time, Richard Dawkins might also be placed in this conflict category given his arguing for, in his words, "militant" atheism and against religious belief in *The God Delusion* (Dawkins 2006); via his eponymous foundation (*https://richarddawkins.net*); and through his association with other well-known atheists such as Sam Harris, Daniel Dennett, and the late Christopher Hitchens, who have referred to themselves as the new atheists.

From the other side, some have argued that science ultimately leads to a purely materialistic or naturalistic worldview, a philosophical position known as scientism. Charles Hodge, a nationally prominent scholar from the Princeton Theological Seminary, made such an assertion in a widely read essay (Hodge 1874) published shortly after *On the Origin of Species*. He equated Darwin's ideas with atheism and strenuously opposed a strictly scientific view of the world. R. Albert Mohler (2005), president of the Southern Baptist Theological Seminary, made similar assertions in a more contemporary editorial.

Independence

The independence approach is somewhat more nuanced and suggests that science and religion are simply two separate domains that should not have any border transgressions. This is a common stance, and I often hear the assertion that science answers "how" questions about the natural world whereas "why" questions about morality and meaning are better left to religious beliefs. Theologian Langdon Gilkey, for example, used this approach during his testimony at the *McLean v. Arkansas* trial (see Chapter 3 for more about this and other court cases) that deemed creation science unconstitutional in 1981 (Barbour 1997).

Another respected voice for this position, particularly among contemporary scientists, was Stephen Jay Gould (1999) and his notion of science and religion as "non-overlapping magisteria." He rejected the warfare thesis, but he understood why it persisted due to essential differences between science and religion:

> I do not see how science and religion could be unified, or even synthesized, under any common scheme of explanation or analysis; but I also do not understand why the two enterprises should experience any conflict. Science tries to document the factual character of the natural world, and to develop theories that coordinate and explain these facts. Religion, on the other hand, operates in the equally important, but utterly

different, realm of human purposes, meanings, and values—subjects that the factual domain of science might illuminate, but can never resolve. (Gould 1999, pp. 4–5)

Many university scientists that I know take Gould's practical approach by making it clear at the beginning of the semester that only science, and not religion, will be discussed. Ecklund (2010, p. 87) referred to this as the "no God on the quad" strategy.

Integration

Integration asserts that common ground must actively be sought and established when conflict is perceived between one's scientific and religious perspectives. Within theological circles, for example, Saint Augustine (2002) asserted that accommodating interpretations of scripture with contemporary knowledge of the world was necessary for maintaining a vibrant religious faith. He argued further that overlooking this accommodation would be mutually detrimental to both faith and reason.

Other Christian theologians such as Thomas Aquinas and Martin Luther advocated for similar two-books approaches (referring to the Book of Nature and the Book of Scripture), as did scientists like Galileo, Newton, and Boyle. Charles Darwin was influenced by such thinking after reading William Paley's *Natural Theology* (1802), where he reconciled his religious beliefs with the vast expansion of scientific knowledge in the 18th and 19th centuries. Let's not forget that Darwin studied to be a minister before turning his attention to natural history.

Like many scientists from the past, Francis Collins (2006), current director of the National Institutes of Health, and Kenneth Miller (2007), cell biologist and public advocate for evolution, view their scientific work as a form of worship and argue for the general consistency of science and their religious faith. I often direct students to these two scientists, and the following statement from Collins (2007) is something I recite in every science-religion course that I teach:

> *But why couldn't this [evolution] be God's plan for creation? True, this is incompatible with an ultra-literal interpretation of Genesis, but long before Darwin, there were many thoughtful interpreters like St. Augustine, who found it impossible to be exactly sure what the meaning of that amazing creation story was supposed to be. So attaching oneself to such literal interpretations in the face of compelling scientific evidence pointing to the ancient age of Earth and the relatedness of living things by evolution seems neither wise nor necessary for the believer. I have found there is a wonderful harmony in the complementary truths of science and faith. The God of the Bible is also the God of the genome. God can be found in the cathedral or in the laboratory. By investigating God's majestic and awesome creation, science can actually be a means of worship.*

Dialogue

Looking back into history, as Collins recognizes, lies at the heart of science-religion dialogue. This last approach does not go as far as strict integration, but it suggests that scientific and religious worldviews should continuously communicate and learn about one another's histories, underlying assumptions, and methods of inquiry. Scholars often favor dialogue, because the actual interactions between science and religion are more historically and culturally conditioned than other categories might suggest. The Galileo affair, for example, was influenced more by the strained relationship between Galileo and Pope Urban VIII and political circumstances during the Protestant Reformation and less by outrage in the Catholic Church over heliocentrism and geokineticism (Barbour 1997). When geology became a formal discipline in 17th-century Europe, some used evidence from fossils and strata to disprove the Genesis account of creation whereas others saw evidence of a worldwide flood described by many ancient mythologies. Thus, dialogue is, in essence, not a stand-alone category, but rather a reminder to treat science-religion relationships with appropriate complexity.

Framework as Starting Point

Barbour's framework has given me a much needed and calming perspective about science-religion interactions and I am a better, more empathetic teacher as a result. My students, like me once upon a time, are sometimes skeptical that science and religion can be discussed in a relational way. Others simply assume ongoing and irreconcilable conflict whereas some, like an acquaintance at a recent social gathering, are incredulous that I discuss topics that are best kept apart. History challenges each of these categorical responses, and even Barbour acknowledged that his framework was only a useful starting point for discussion. Those well versed in the history and philosophy of science will recognize that much more nuance can be added to any of the above examples. Historical case studies, however, help us to realize that many of the same questions about science and religion have been asked and will continue to be revisited in new contexts. Even a modest foundation in history can help our students, communities, and ourselves to develop more mature understandings about science and religion.

EVOLUTION AS THE ESSENTIAL SCIENCE-RELIGION CASE STUDY

Until 12 years ago, I had little understanding about either the general tenets of evolutionary theory or why there seemed to be a never-ending controversy about teaching evolution in public schools. As a chemist, I had little exposure to evolution during my education and the issue hardly arose during my first career as a high school teacher. The *Kitzmiller* trial, Barbour (1997), and biology students in my science methods courses, however, changed all of that. I now take evolution much more seriously, and in this section I summarize what I have learned about the historical origins of anti-evolution sentiments in the United States.

Barbour (1997) reminds us that Darwin's ideas were rapidly and widely accepted in scientific circles in the decades following the publication of *On the Origin of Species*. Natural selection based on variation in physical traits and population-level thinking helped biology develop from a largely descriptive field to one with an explanatory and predictive theoretical framework. In brief, Darwin forever changed how we view the natural world, and it is unusual in the history of science to see ideas spread so quickly and especially during the lifetimes of scientists who propose such radical departures from conventional wisdom.

Immediate reactions from theologians and religious leaders, however, were understandably mixed, and Darwin was well aware of the implications that his ideas would have for religious adherents. In fact, he delayed publication of *On the Origin of Species* for nearly 14 years largely because of these concerns. Many of Darwin's contemporaries opted to follow Augustine's doctrine of accommodation and asserted that natural selection was one mechanism through which a supernatural creator interacted with the physical world—an approach referred to as theistic evolution, which can safely be placed in the integration camp. Others perpetuated the conflict thesis by arguing that evolution denied the existence of a supernatural creator and necessarily led to atheism and a strict materialist worldview.

Shortly after Darwin's death in 1882, controversies around evolution largely receded as most scientists and many theologians in Europe and the United States became convinced by the preponderance of empirical evidence independently gathered from a variety of scientific disciplines. Many Christians, for example, altered their theological beliefs by interpreting the six days in Genesis as extended geologic epochs, which is referred to as the day-age approach. Broadly speaking, science and religion appeared to have made their peace with Darwin's ideas.

As detailed by Marsden (2006), circumstances in the United States changed abruptly at the turn of the 20th century, particularly in the aftermath of World War I. A far-reaching, interdenominational Christian movement coalesced to reject much of contemporary theological scholarship, to dispute the notion of science as a progressive social force, and to reaffirm what leaders asserted were American Christianity's core beliefs. Aptly named the Fundamentalist movement after a 12-volume series entitled *The Fundamentals* and because of organizations such as the World's Christian Fundamentals Association, large numbers of American Christians rallied behind three complementary concepts: dispensational premillennialism, naïve or strict literalism, and biblical inerrancy.

Brief definitions are useful to know: Dispensational premillennialism suggests that society currently exists in the sixth of seven ages or dispensations to be followed by the millennium, an apocalyptic period of reckoning by a supernatural creator. Naïve or strictly literal interpretations hold that scriptural truth is evident in the surface appearance of words and syntax. A Fundamentalist interpretation tends to reject modern biblical criticism that views much of scripture as mythology, allegory, and metaphor. Biblical inerrancy suggests that Christian scripture must be viewed as completely and historically (and scientifically in some cases) accurate as written.

Each tenet has unique origins and is emphasized to varying degrees depending on the person or religious organization. One takeaway is that Christian Fundamentalism was a profound historical movement in the United States that is rarely taught in schools. Consequently, we may not understand how aspects of Fundamentalism are still with us today in science classrooms. At the onset, Fundamentalism was a reaction against industrialization, urbanization, immigration, public education, and critical analysis of Christian scripture. Evolution was caught up in the backlash, and opposition to its teaching became a centerpiece of the movement. Marsden's emphasis on the anti-evolution nature of Fundamentalism is noteworthy for all science teachers:

> The meteoric rise of the anti-evolution issue—which was closely connected with the World War I notion of saving civilization from German theology and its superman philosophy—was swiftly transforming the character of the fundamentalist movement, particularly in its premillennialist branch, which found that a social and political question was now virtually its first concern. This transformation was involved with an immense surge in popularity; the anti-evolution movement was becoming a national fad. Both the premillennial movement and denominational fundamentalism had been confined mostly to Northern states, but anti-evolution swept through the South and found new constituencies in rural areas everywhere. Many people with little or no interest in fundamentalism's doctrinal concerns were drawn into the campaign to keep Darwinism out of America's schools. (Marsden 2006, p. 170)

Thus, for followers of Fundamentalism as well as for influential leaders such as Charles Hodge and William Jennings Bryan (Kazin 2006), one of the prosecuting attorneys in the 1925 Scopes trial, opposition to evolution was precisely an article of religious faith.

Marsden's book and, in particular, the above quote marked another turning point for me. I recall feeling genuine angst after understanding the roots of Fundamentalism and its inherently anti-evolution subculture. I was also rather dismayed to learn that my own denomination had contributed to and eventually split over issues in what was known as the fundamentalist-modernist controversy (Longfield 1991).

Unlike Barbour's framework, the history behind Christian Fundamentalism in the United States was far more daunting for me to study and accept. Although I have neither self-identified as a fundamentalist nor been raised in this tradition, I routinely hear echoes of the movement in regional churches, among university students, and even from science teachers on occasion. As Chapter 3 will elaborate, Fundamentalism-inspired, anti-evolution rhetoric still exists and a few well-financed institutions continue to undermine evolutionary theory and other scientific concepts and thus make our jobs as science teachers that much more challenging.

GENERAL ADVICE REGARDING SCIENCE-RELIGION HISTORY

Even with the historical perspective I have gained in recent years, I still get upset when I revisit *Kitzmiller* and follow the dozens of subsequent attempts by states, school boards, and even some teachers to undermine evolution in particular, and science in general. In the grander scheme beyond the courtroom and beyond evolution, I have learned that there is no substitute for being versed in history when responding to questions and concerns about science-religion relationships. Science teachers who are conversant in how the concepts they teach have been received by religious communities are, in my view, well on their way to responsibly addressing what often seems like an intractable problem.

I conclude here with some general advice to my fellow science educators and to all who support quality science education. Unlike many chapters in this book, those from Part II in particular, I do not offer specific ideas for classroom teaching, but rather some parting shots and resources for your consideration.

My first piece of advice is the same as most historians'. Get the history right. In addition to Barbour (1997) and Marsden (2006), I recommend Larson's (1998, 2002) definitive history of the Scopes trial and lectures on evolution, Numbers's (2006) and Scott's (2004) accounts of various forms of creationism, and Principe's (2006) historical overview of science and religion. *The Oxford Handbook of Religion and Science* (Clayton and Simpson 2006) or archived videos from the Gifford Lectures on natural theology (*www.giffordlectures.org*) are not for the faint of heart, but they will give you a sense of the depth of available

> "There is a strong precedent for viewing science and religion as complementary and for reconciling understandings of the natural, material world with metaphysical, spiritual traditions."

scholarship. Simple internet searches will reveal videos by many of these authors, and they tend to be more accessible and appropriate for lay audiences.

Second, understand that religiously motivated opposition to science is only one chapter in the long science-religion story. There is, in fact, a strong precedent for viewing science and religion as complementary and for reconciling understandings of the natural, material world with metaphysical, spiritual traditions. As a perusal of the *Oxford Handbook* (Clayton and Simpson 2006) illustrates, monotheistic traditions such as Christianity, Judaism, and Islam often view science as a form of worship leading to greater understanding of their creator's activity in the world. More plural or nontheistic religions (e.g., Hinduism, Buddhism, religions of indigenous populations) tend to emphasize the pursuit of truth and peaceful coexistence with one another and with nature. Within such traditions, science is one pathway to these ends.

Official statements from contemporary religious institutions reinforce this historical trajectory. The *MIT Survey on Science, Religion, and Origins* (Lee, Tegmark, and Chita-Tegmark 2013), for example, indicates that only 11% of religious groups openly and knowingly reject some aspect of science (e.g., evolution, Big Bang cosmology) due to the alleged inconsistencies with their interpretations of sacred texts. The vast majority of religious institutions embrace scientific inquiry. I was, for example, delighted when my denomination strengthened its support in 2016 (National Center for Science Education 2016).

Third and lastly, get your story straight and encourage others to do the same. Regardless of your personal background, take the time to articulate a responsible relationship between scientific and religious, spiritual, and/or metaphysical points of view. Care must be taken, of course, to neither advocate nor denigrate a particular religion in public settings (see Chapter 4 for legal considerations), but there is no reason to avoid the science-religion discussion. This can serve to build trust and rapport with students, colleagues, and community members.

Fortunately, there are numerous resources and examples available to us. I highly recommend the American Association for the Advancement of Science's (2017) Dialogue on Science, Ethics, and Religion (DoSER) initiative. DoSER has "facilitate[d] communication between scientific and religious communities" since 1995 and is the program that directly engages these issues at the world's largest science society. *The Evolution Dialogues* (Baker and Miller 2006) is just one example of its work, and it has developed a Science for Seminaries project in consultation with the Association of Theological Schools.

Academic institutions such as the Zygon Center for Religion and Science (*http://zygoncenter.org*), Berkeley's Center for Theology and the Natural Sciences (*www.ctns.org*), and the Center for the Study of Science in Muslim Societies (*www.hampshire.edu/ssims/center-for-the-study-of-science-in-muslim-societies*) are worth exploring. The National Center for Science Education (*www.ncse.com*) includes science-religion interactions within its mission to defend the teaching of evolution and climate science.

Additionally, many faith-based organizations are devoted to reconciling their specific theologies, beliefs, and practices with science. Biologos (*http://biologos.org*), cofounded by Francis Collins, and the American Scientific Affiliation (*http://network.asa3.org*) are particularly useful for understanding Christian perspectives. The McGill Centre for Islam and Science (*www.islam-and-science.org*) has resources from a Muslim point of view.

So, the resources are there. The need to address science and religion in a responsible manner is pressing given the accelerating pace of scientific discovery and the continued religiosity of our culture and student population. I will now leave it up to you to choose the next steps. Perhaps you will include science-religion interactions as part of a NOS or biography-of-a-scientist lesson. A joint project with a social studies teacher to explore the scientific and social implications of Darwin's ideas is another possibility. It would not be too labor intensive to organize a panel discussion about reconciling science and religion as part of International Darwin Day celebrations. You and your colleagues could preempt students' concerns by developing a departmental position statement on scientific concepts that might conflict with religious beliefs. My colleagues in subsequent chapters will certainly provide you with additional ideas.

Throughout this book, we make the argument that science-religion interactions are to be taken seriously. It is a worthwhile intellectual pursuit, but it has the potential to be much more than that. You already know the science, and many of you have probably grappled with how your scientific knowledge relates to your spiritual beliefs regardless of their connection to a specific religious tradition. We have all encountered students with serious concerns or even objections to what we teach. What better group of boundary pioneers is there than their science teachers?

REFERENCES

American Association for the Advancement of Science. 2017. Dialogue on Science, Ethics, and Religion. *www.aaas.org/DoSER.*

Baker, C., and J. B. Miller. 2006. *The evolution dialogues: Science, Christianity, and the quest for understanding.* Washington, DC: American Association for the Advancement of Science.

Barbour, I. G. 1997. *Religion and science: Historical and contemporary issues.* New York: HarperCollins.

Clayton, P., and Z. Simpson. 2006. *The Oxford handbook of religion and science.* New York: Oxford University Press.

Collins, F. S. 2006. *The language of God: A scientist presents evidence for belief.* New York: Simon and Schuster.

Collins, F. S. 2007. Why this scientist believes in God. CNN.com. *www.cnn.com/2007/US/04/03/collins. commentary/index.html.*

Darwin, C. 1859. *On the origin of species.* Cambridge, MA: Harvard University Press.

Dawkins, R. 2006. *The God delusion.* New York: Houghton Mifflin.

Draper, J. W. 1876. *A history of the conflict between religion and science.* New York: Appleton.

Ecklund, E. H. 2010. *Science vs. religion: What scientists really think.* New York: Oxford University Press.

Gould, S. J. 1999. *Rocks of ages: Science and religion in the fullness of life.* New York: Ballantine.

Hodge, C. 1874. What is Darwinism? Project Gutenberg. *www.gutenberg.org/files/19192/19192-h/19192-h.htm.*

Jones, J. E. 2005. Memorandum opinion for the *Kitzmiller v. Dover Area School District* trial. *http:// ncse.com/files/pub/legal/kitzmiller/highlights/2005-12-20_Kitzmiller_decision.pdf.*

Kazin, M. 2006. *A godly hero: The life of William Jennings Bryan.* New York: Anchor Books.

Larson, E. J. 1998. *Summer for the gods: The Scopes trial and America's continuing debate over science and religion.* Cambridge, MA: Harvard University Press.

Larson, E. J. 2002. *The theory of evolution: A history of controversy.* Chantilly, VA: The Teaching Company.

Lee, E., M. Tegmark, and M. Chita-Tegmark. 2013. The MIT survey on science, religion, and origins: The belief gap. MIT Kavli Institute. *http://space.mit.edu/home/tegmark/survey.html.*

Longfield, B. L. 1991. *The Presbyterian controversy: Fundamentalists, modernists, and moderates.* New York: Oxford University Press.

Marsden, G. M. 2006. *Fundamentalism and American culture.* New York: Oxford University Press.

Miller, K. R. 2007. *Finding Darwin's God: A scientist's search for common ground between God and evolution.* New York: Harper Perennial.

Mohler, R. A. 2005. The origins of life: An evangelical Baptist view. NPR.org. *www.npr.org/templates/story/story.php?storyId=4760816.*

National Center for Science Education. 2005. *Kitzmiller v. Dover:* Intelligent design on trial. *https://ncse.com/library-resource/kitzmiller-v-dover-intelligent-design-trial.*

National Center for Science Education. 2016. Presbyterian Church (USA). *https://ncse.com/library-resource/presbyterian-church-usa.*

Numbers, R. L. 2006. *The creationists: From scientific creationism to intelligent design.* Cambridge, MA: Harvard University Press.

Paley, W. 1802. *Natural theology.* New York: Oxford University Press.

Principe, L. M. 2006. *Science and religion.* Chantilly, VA: The Teaching Company.

Saint Augustine. 2002. *The works of Saint Augustine: A translation for the 21st century.* Hyde Park, NY: New City Press.

Scott, E. C. 2004. *Evolution vs. creationism: An introduction.* Berkeley, CA: University of California Press.

Shane, J. W. 2019. An evolving interdisciplinary seminar on science and religion. *Honors in Practice* 15: 79–94.

Wikipedia contributors. 2019. Kitzmiller v. Dover Area School District. *Wikipedia*, July 29. *https://en.wikipedia.org/w/index.php?title=Kitzmiller_v._Dover_Area_School_District&oldid=908459594.*

The Arc of History Bends Toward Teaching Evolution

Barbara Forrest

Teaching evolution has presented a challenge to American teachers since the 1920s. Some, fearing controversy, avoid the subject completely while others devote as little time to it as possible (Berkman and Plutzer 2011). Even those who teach it enthusiastically usually expect resistance from creationist students, parents, or community members. Yet proper science education requires instruction in evolutionary theory. Science teachers can, and are obligated to, teach evolution supported by the knowledge that their instruction is being constantly reinforced by a vast and ever-increasing body of evidence. However, teachers may be surprised to learn that proper science education is supported by more than the science that forms the basis of their curriculum. It is also supported, paradoxically, by the history of creationism itself.

Through my own work as a scholar and activist, I have gained an insider's perspective on this history. From 1994 to 1996, I worked successfully to prevent the adoption of a creationist curriculum guide in my children's school district (Forrest 1997). I served on the Board of Directors of both the American Civil Liberties Union in Louisiana (1995–1997) and the National Center for Science Education (2004–2017), a clearinghouse for assistance in protecting science education. As an academic, my scholarly research about the intelligent design (ID) creationist movement resulted in my serving as an expert witness in the first legal case involving ID (*Kitzmiller et al. v. Dover Area School District* 2005).

While the history of creationism in America is most fundamentally the history of religious (specifically, Protestant fundamentalist and evangelical) opposition to evolution, another facet of it, often obscured by creationists' attention-grabbing antics, is too frequently overlooked. An accurate history of creationism necessarily highlights the pro-science community's successes in beating back creationists' efforts either to prevent or to undermine the teaching of evolution. Setbacks notwithstanding, these successes have created a period of relative stability that is giving teachers, scientists, and pro-science activists time to help advance greater science literacy among students and the public. There is also evidence that American social and political attitudes are changing in ways that point to greater acceptance of sound science education, especially the teaching of evolution.

HISTORY OF AMERICAN CREATIONISM: FROM CREATIONISM TO CREATION SCIENCE TO INTELLIGENT DESIGN

To some extent, the history of creationism is part of American common knowledge. Many people know about the 1925 Scopes Monkey Trial in Dayton, Tennessee, in which John Scopes was convicted for teaching evolution in the local public high school. That trial was the result of the Tennessee legislature's March 23, 1925, passage of the Butler Act, making it illegal for public school teachers to teach "any theory that denies the Story of Divine Creation of man as taught in the Bible, and to teach instead that man has descended from a lower order of animal" (Scott 2009, p. 99). Scopes was convicted, and although the Tennessee Supreme Court later overturned his conviction on a technicality (Scott 2009), teaching evolution in Tennessee public schools remained illegal under the Butler Act.

Despite Scopes's conviction, legal victory came at a steep price for creationists. Defense attorney Clarence Darrow's devastating—and widely publicized—cross-examination of prosecuting attorney William Jennings Bryan left biblical creationism in tatters, making evolution the winner by default in the court of public opinion (despite the fact that none of Darrow's expert witnesses in science and theology were permitted to testify) (Scott 2009). However, although the general consensus at the time was that the trial elevated the scientific status of evolution, this consensus did not produce any beneficial effects on science curricula in the United States. In fact, as far as evolution was concerned, science education actually got worse, as I will describe shortly. Yet, paradoxically, just as the public relations setback for biblical creationism did not result in better science education, the legal victory for creationists in Tennessee state court did not portend their future success in the federal courts. The legal victory in Tennessee turned out to be an outlier rather than a precedent, as later challenges in federal courts would prove. But this turn of events was still decades away.

After the Scopes trial, although other states tried and failed to pass legislation similar to Tennessee's Butler Act, both Mississippi and Arkansas succeeded, passing their own anti-evolution laws in 1926 and 1928, respectively (Moore 2002). Arkansas enacted its law by means of a ballot initiative in 1928, becoming the only state ever to enact an anti-evolution statute by popular vote (*Epperson v. Arkansas* 1968; Ledbetter 1979; Moore 2002). These laws, along with the Butler Act, remained in effect until the 1960s, when they were finally challenged in federal court (Scott 2009). After the Scopes trial, the number of high school teachers who taught evolution actually dropped lower than before, and evolution began to disappear from textbooks nationwide (Scott 2009). In fact, the acceptance of creationism eclipsed the teaching of evolution so quickly and effectively that "by 1930, only five years after the Scopes trial, an estimated 70 percent of American classrooms omitted evolution" (Scott 2009, p. 103). This situation lasted for almost four decades, until the first successful federal court challenge in 1968.

In the 1950s, world events forced a change in American science education. When the Soviets successfully launched the *Sputnik* satellite in 1957, Americans were shocked into the realization that American science education was seriously outdated, placing the United States at a competitive disadvantage. As a result, the National Science Foundation funded the Biological Sciences Curriculum Study (BSCS), from which emerged in the early 1960s a completely revamped approach to teaching biology, supported by new textbooks presenting evolution "as an indispensable component of the biological sciences that students must understand to understand biology fully" (Scott 2009, p. 104). The BSCS textbooks proved popular with school boards nationwide. The inclusion of evolution also generated a creationist backlash that sparked a resurgence of efforts to counteract the teaching of evolution in public schools. However, 40 years after the Scopes trial, these efforts also set the stage for a consistent series of legal defeats for creationists in the federal courts.

Beginning with the first federal court defeat in 1968, creationism began to evolve in a way that reflects this legal history. Yet, its evolution has been tactical and linguistic rather than substantive. From a tactical standpoint, creationists were forced to stop trying to ban the teaching of evolution and began trying instead to get creationism into public schools alongside evolution. When that failed, they began devising strategies to undermine the teaching of evolution, an effort that continues today. From a linguistic standpoint, creationists are attempting to conceal their identity and disguise their curricular proposals by altering their terminology in order to evade constitutional constraints (Forrest 2008, 2010).

A BRIEF LEGAL HISTORY

The legal history of creationism is the history of adaptation in response to defeat. The blatant biblical creationism of the 1920s became "creation science" in the 1960s in response to the reintroduction of evolution in the BSCS curricula and textbooks (Scott 2009). After legal defeats in the 1980s, creation science became "intelligent design" (Forrest 2010). Following the most recent federal court defeat in 2005 (*Kitzmiller et al. v. Dover*), ID has morphed into a litany of code phrases such as teaching the "evidence for and against evolution" and "critical analysis" of evolution, reflecting ID proponents' effort to deflect attention from the creationist substance of ID (Forrest 2010). One truly remarkable fact about the consistently successful legal challenges that have blocked the teaching of creationism since the 1960s is that in each case, teachers, either individuals or teacher organizations, stood up and served as primary plaintiffs.

> *"One truly remarkable fact about the consistently successful legal challenges that have blocked the teaching of creationism since the 1960s is that in each case, teachers stood up and served as primary plaintiffs."*

Along with Tennessee, Arkansas was among a handful of southern states whose 1920s-era laws banning the teaching of evolution remained in effect after the Scopes trial. The adoption of the BSCS science curricula and the prominent inclusion of evolution in text-books consequently put teachers in these states at odds with the law. When the Arkansas Education Association decided to challenge it, high school biology teacher Susan Epperson became the lead plaintiff, arguing that the law violated the Establishment Clause of the First Amendment of the U.S. Constitution and Epperson's right under the Arkansas Constitution to "free communication of thoughts and opinions" as an instructor (Moore 2002, p. 48).

After Epperson won in the Arkansas Chancery Court, the Arkansas Supreme Court overturned the ruling. When the case was appealed to the U.S. Supreme Court in *Epperson v. Arkansas* (1968), the court ruled in Epperson's favor, declaring that the Arkansas law violated the First Amendment's prohibition of the establishment of religion and deprived Epperson of her right to due process under the Fourteenth Amendment (Moore 2002, p. 56):

> *In the present case, there can be no doubt that Arkansas has sought to prevent its teachers from discussing the theory of evolution because it is contrary to the belief of some that the Book of Genesis must be the exclusive source of doctrine as to the origin of man. ... Arkansas did not seek to excise from the curricula of its schools and universities all discussion of the origin of man. The law's effort was confined to an attempt to blot out a particular theory because of its supposed conflict with the Biblical account, literally read. Plainly, the law is contrary to the mandate of the First, and in violation of the Fourteenth, Amendments to the Constitution.*

Creationists were forced to regroup after *Epperson*, which struck down the Arkansas law, and thus all state laws, banning evolution: "The law must be stricken because of its conflict with the constitutional prohibition of state laws respecting an establishment of religion or prohibiting the free exercise thereof. ... Government in our democracy, state and national, must be neutral in matters of religious theory, doctrine, and practice" (*Epperson v. Arkansas* 1968). Consequently, because creationists had failed to get evolution out of public schools, the strategy was now aimed at getting equal time for creationism *inside* them (Numbers 1982).

In the 1970s, proponents of creationism rebranded it as "creation science" in an effort to portray it as a scientific theory on a par with evolutionary theory, adopting their "two-model" approach (Numbers 1982). However, creation science was still grounded in the biblical literalism of American Protestant Fundamentalism (see Chapter 2), and the changes were tactical and cosmetic rather than substantive. Consequently, the pitch to school boards was crafted accordingly, as the following instructions to creationists in the March 1980 *Bible Science Newsletter* make clear: "Sell more SCIENCE. ... Do not use the word 'creation.' Speak only of science. Explain that withholding information contradicting evolution amounts to 'censorship' and smacks of getting into the province of religious dogma. ... Use the 'censorship' label as one who is against censoring science. YOU are for science" (Numbers

1982, p. 543). (As will be seen below, this strategy of verbal subterfuge remains in use.) According to Ronald L. Numbers, a historian of creationism, "This tactic proved extremely effective. Two state legislatures and various school boards adopted the two-model approach" (Numbers 1982, p. 543). Those two state legislatures were Arkansas and Louisiana.

The Arkansas and Louisiana laws were both adopted in 1981. Arkansas Act 590, entitled the Balanced Treatment for Creation-Science and Evolution-Science Act, mandated "instruction in both scientific models (of evolution-science and creation-science) if public schools choose to teach either" (Arkansas Act 590, 1981, p. 12). On May 27, 1981, the American Civil Liberties Union filed suit in federal court, with teacher organizations serving as plaintiffs, along with religious organizations, civil liberties groups, and individuals (McLean Documentation Project 2005). On January 5, 1982, after a widely publicized trial, U.S. District Court Judge William R. Overton issued his ruling in *McLean v. Arkansas Board of Education* (1982), declaring Act 590 to be an unconstitutional establishment of religion and thus in violation of the First Amendment of the U.S. Constitution. Overton concluded his decision by affirming that "no group, no matter how large or small, may use the organs of government, of which the public schools are the most conspicuous and influential, to foist its religious beliefs on others" (*McLean v. Arkansas* 1982).

Although *McLean v. Arkansas* was binding only on public schools in the Eastern District of Arkansas, Overton's thorough, carefully crafted opinion reverberated nationwide, not the least because of his clear, concise description of the nature of science (which is consistent with other descriptions provided in this book; see Chapter 1). Overton stated, "More precisely, the essential characteristics of science are: (1) It is guided by natural law; (2) It has to be explanatory by reference to natural law; (3) It is testable against the empirical world; (4) Its conclusions are tentative, i.e., are not necessarily the final word; and (5) It is falsifiable" (*McLean v. Arkansas* 1982). The strength of Overton's reasoning discouraged the state of Arkansas from appealing the decision (Scott 2009). Louisiana, however, had been following the *McLean v. Arkansas* case closely.

Louisiana Senate Bill No. 86 mirrored Arkansas Act 590 in almost all respects, including the title, the Balanced Treatment for Creation-Science and Evolution-Science Act (Louisiana Senate Bill No. 86, 1981). Both laws also cited protection of academic freedom as a primary purpose (Arkansas Act 590, 1981; Louisiana Senate Bill No. 86, 1981). However, the *McLean v. Arkansas* case persuaded the authors of Senate Bill 86 to sanitize its language somewhat in an attempt to avoid similar legal pitfalls. Act 590's definition of creation science—which included "sudden creation of the universe, energy, and life from nothing," "separate ancestry for man and apes," and "explanation of the earth's geology by catastrophism, including the occurrence of a worldwide flood"—was clearly based on Genesis. Consequently, the authors of Senate Bill 86 defined creation science merely as "the scientific evidences for creation and inferences from those scientific evidences" (Louisiana Senate Bill No. 86, 1981).

In addition, whereas Arkansas Act 590 was mandatory, stating that "this Act does not require any instruction in the subject of origins, but simply requires instruction in both scientific models (of evolution-science and creation-science) if public schools choose to teach either" (Arkansas Act 590, 1981, p. 12), Louisiana Senate Bill 86 was worded so as to appear merely permissive: "This Subpart [of LA Revised Statute 17:286] does not require any instruction in the subject of origins but simply *permits* instruction in both models … if public schools choose to teach either" (Louisiana Senate Bill No. 86, 1981, p. 1314) (emphasis added). Ultimately, however, this strategy failed.

In December 1981, the American Civil Liberties Union filed a federal lawsuit challenging Louisiana Senate Bill 86, which had come to be known as the Balanced Treatment Act. As in *Epperson v. Arkansas*, teachers were at the forefront. Don Aguillard, an Acadiana High School biology teacher in Lafayette, Louisiana, was the lead plaintiff in a list that included five teacher organizations (*Aguillard v. Treen* 1983; Moore 2002). The case eventually reached the U.S. Supreme Court, which, in a 7-2 vote (with Justices Antonin Scalia and William Rehnquist dissenting), ruled that the Balanced Treatment Act was an unconstitutional establishment of religion: "The Act is facially invalid as violative of the Establishment Clause of the First Amendment, because it lacks a clear secular purpose" (*Edwards v. Aguillard* 1987).

The declaration that Louisiana Senate Bill 86 was "facially invalid" meant that its language was enough to establish its unconstitutionality without any actual application of the law; its relatively sanitized language could not conceal the fact that *creation* is by its nature a religious term. The court ruled that "the Act impermissibly endorses religion by advancing the religious belief that a supernatural being created humankind" and recognized its religious purpose: "The legislative history demonstrates that the term 'creation science,' as contemplated by the state legislature, embraces this religious teaching. The Act's primary purpose was to change the public school science curriculum to provide persuasive advantage to a particular religious doctrine that rejects the factual basis of evolution in its entirety" (*Edwards v. Aguillard* 1987). Moreover, the court rejected the "academic freedom" rationale: "The Act does not further its stated secular purpose of 'protecting academic freedom.' It does not enhance the freedom of teachers to teach what they choose, and fails to further the goal of 'teaching all of the evidence'" (*Edwards v. Aguillard* 1987). More than three decades later, however, "academic freedom" is one of the code phrases being used by ID creationists.

With the goal of getting creation science into public schools no longer viable, creationists had to shift their strategy yet again. The only tactic that remained to them was the merely cosmetic one of renaming creation science and abandoning its most overtly fundamentalist (that is, biblical literalist) characteristics, namely, the young age of the Earth (6,000–10,000 years) and Noah's flood, on which their "flood geology" was based (Scott 2009). William Bennetta, a biologist and watchdog who founded the Textbook League in order to sound the alarm about attacks on science education and textbooks (Branch 2018), wrote a contemporary account of the Louisiana Balanced Treatment Act. In 1988, he explained the origin and ultimate fate of the law while presciently predicting exactly the strategy that creationists subsequently adopted (and that ID creationists still use when addressing mainstream audiences):

> Because the term "creation-science" has been sullied … in Edwards v. Aguillard, the creationists' new pseudoscience will carry a new name, or perhaps several new names. Its content will be fully sterilized: it will avoid explicit supernaturalism, and it will speak not of any god but of a nebulous "intelligence" or "intelligent cause." It will be much more sophisticated than orthodox "creation-science" because it will shun created "kinds," a worldwide flood, and other topics that clearly point to episodes in the Bible. Its literature will avoid blatant references to the literature of orthodox "creation-science" and will be untainted by any obvious connections to fundamentalist ministries or to fundamentalist publishers. (Bennetta 1988)

This strategy got underway as soon as the *Edwards v. Aguillard* ruling became public, and the new creationism was again rebranded, this time as "intelligent design" (Forrest 2010). Bennetta correctly predicted that creationists would discard overt references to Genesis. However, ID, which is a form of old-Earth creationism, retains all of the other identifiable elements of creationism: denial of common ancestry, the misinterpretation of purported gaps in the fossil record, and so on. (Forrest and Gross 2007). Moreover, ID is also biblically based. Seeking to avoid political strain between themselves and young-Earth creationists, the ID movement's founders base ID on the New Testament Gospel of John rather than on Genesis (while, for public relations purposes, denying to the media and mainstream audiences that ID is based on the Bible) (Forrest and Gross 2007).

In addition to the shift in strategy and nomenclature, creationism's organizational center shifted from young-Earth organizations such as the Institute for Creation Research to the ID movement, which is headquartered at the Discovery Institute, a conservative think tank in Seattle, Washington (Forrest and Gross 2007). Just as important, the political center of power moved from fundamentalist Christians to evangelicals, who were more politically savvy, more sophisticated, and better organized. In fact, the transformation of creation science into ID coincided with the political ascent of Christian evangelicals in the United States in the 1980s (Forrest and Gross 2007; McVicar 2016).

Because the *Edwards v. Aguillard* ruling meant that young-Earth creationism was no longer legally viable, the power shift from Protestant fundamentalists to ID creationists, who are predominantly evangelical Christians, was highly significant (see Chapter 2 for additional information about the Christian Fundamentalist movement). Fundamentalists are distinguished from evangelicals by the former's tendency toward biblical literalism and other factors such as their reluctance to accommodate mainstream culture. Evangelicals, though, while believing that the Bible is "inerrant" (without factual error) in every respect, interpret scripture in more nuanced ways and are more willing to interact with mainstream culture to spread their religious message and to advance their cultural and political goals more broadly (Green 2004).

While the term *evangelical* is somewhat nebulous and includes both conservative and progressive Christians who disagree sharply on social and political issues, the word has come to be associated almost exclusively since the 1970s with a subset of Christians who believe in being born again, carrying the message of Christianity to mainstream culture in order to counteract secularism, and achieving influence over public policy in order to shape it according to their beliefs. They are overwhelmingly Protestant, although they include Catholics. This subset of Christians is referred to collectively as the Religious Right because they are religiously and politically conservative and have typically aligned themselves with the Republican Party (Green 2004; Pew Research Center 2015c).

Evangelicals consider it their mission to, as they put it, engage modern culture in order to influence policy in areas that include public education. They tend to be better educated, more urban, and more affluent than fundamentalists. Like fundamentalists, they believe that the Bible is inerrant; however, they are more flexible in their interpretation of scripture and more willing than fundamentalists to seek the political power that will enable them to enact their beliefs as public policy. To do this, they have adopted many of the trappings of popular culture that fundamentalists shun, such as the use of television, radio, and now the internet and other social media, which, along with their cultivation of political influence, have helped them to move into the American mainstream (Green 2004). By the mid-1990s, the Discovery Institute, which was founded and is run predominantly by evangelicals (Forrest and Gross 2007), was poised to take advantage of the religious power shift in order to promote ID.

The Discovery Institute outlined its strategy for promoting ID in a 1998 document popularly known as the Wedge Document (Forrest and Gross 2007). Its aggressive campaign eventually bore fruit. In 2004, the Board of Directors of the Dover Area School District in Pennsylvania adopted a policy requiring that students "be made aware of gaps/problems in Darwin's theory and of other theories … including … intelligent design" (*Tammy Kitzmiller et al. v. Dover Area School District* 2004, pp. 1–2). The board also required Dover High School biology teachers to read a statement to ninth-grade classes asserting that "intelligent design is an explanation of the origin of life that differs from Darwin's view" and referring students to an ID textbook, *Of Pandas and People* (*Tammy Kitzmiller et al. v. Dover Area School District* 2004). The teachers refused, and 11 parents, 3 of them public school teachers, sued the board, initiating the legal complaint that became the first ID court case, *Tammy Kitzmiller et al. v. Dover Area School District* (2004).

I was an expert witness for the *Kitzmiller v. Dover* plaintiffs. My work and that of other scientists and scholars had thoroughly exposed ID as merely the newest variant of creationism (Forrest and Gross 2007). Consequently, the Discovery Institute, knowing that the term *intelligent design* was a legal liability, urged the board either to sanitize the policy by eliminating the term or to withdraw it altogether. The board refused, and the case went to trial in September 2005.

On December 20, 2005, after six weeks of testimony, Federal District Judge John E. Jones III, recognizing that "ID cannot uncouple itself from its creationist, and thus religious, antecedents," ruled that the policy was a violation of the First Amendment of the U.S. Constitution (*Kitzmiller et al. v. Dover Area School District* 2005). Thus, just as *Epperson v. Arkansas* (1968) prohibited banning evolution from public schools and *Edwards v. Aguillard* (1987) prohibited teaching creation-science, so *Kitzmiller v. Dover* (2005) ended creationists' hope of promoting creationism in the guise of intelligent design. Judge Jones's ruling was binding only in the Middle District of Pennsylvania, but, like Judge Overton's *McLean v. Arkansas Board of Education* ruling, it reverberated nationwide because of Jones's powerful, comprehensive reasoning.

LONG-TERM TRENDS FAVOR TEACHING EVOLUTION

Although the U.S. Constitution has protected the teaching of evolution thus far, creationists' consistent federal court losses do not guarantee future legal victories for science education. While U.S. demographics are changing in ways that appear to favor teaching evolution, the demographics of federal courts are moving in the opposite direction as the Religious Right succeeds in influencing the selection of judges, for whom one litmus test will surely be support for further weakening the separation of church and state (Montgomery 2017). Indeed, the enactment of anti-science policies at the national level by the Donald Trump administration, beginning in 2017 and continuing as of this writing, raises the question of whether pro-science forces are stable enough to withstand the current political climate (Levitan 2017). Nonetheless, signs for the long-term future of science education are encouraging, albeit with periodic setbacks.

One such setback is the adoption of stealth creationist legislation in Louisiana and Tennessee. After the *Kitzmiller v. Dover* verdict in 2005, the Discovery Institute began promoting to state legislatures a model Academic Freedom Act, repurposing the academic freedom rationale of early-1980s balanced treatment laws that the Supreme Court nullified in its 1987 *Edwards v. Aguillard* ruling. Couched in creationist code language, the model bill purported to give teachers permission to undermine evolution by conferring the "right and freedom to present scientific information pertaining to the full range of scientific views regarding biological and chemical evolution" (National Center for Science Education 2009). In 2008, Louisiana became the first state to adopt such legislation, deceptively named the Louisiana Science Education Act (Louisiana Act 473, 2008). Tennessee followed in 2012 when the governor allowed a similar bill to become law without his signature (Branch 2012).

CHAPTER 3

The Discovery Institute's 2015 revised version of its model bill would allow teachers to include "the scientific strengths and scientific weaknesses" of "biological evolution, the chemical origins of life, global warming, and human cloning" in order to develop students' "critical thinking skills" (Discovery Institute, n.d.). The use of code language such as "the full range of scientific views regarding biological and chemical evolution," "critical thinking," and "strengths and weaknesses" of evolution is now the only tactic available to creationists after their court defeats (Forrest 2010, p. 178; Forrest and Gross 2007, p. 337).

Such rhetorical subterfuge is the result of the pro-science community's success to date in beating back creationism. Creationists seem to be losing ground, and support for sound science education seems to be solidifying in states such as Texas where anti-evolutionism has been vigorous. In 2013, Texas creationists failed to influence the Texas State Board of Education's selection of biology textbooks: "Highly placed stakeholders—ranging from those in publishing to sitting board members—believe the culture warriors are losing the ability to run roughshod over state education. … The statewide reach of the culture warriors is ending" (Hargrove 2013). To date, only Louisiana and Tennessee have adopted the Discovery Institute's legislation (Thompson 2012). The Texas legislature rejected it in 2017, with the Board of Education also stripping creationist language from science standards the same year (Branch 2017a, 2017d). Moreover, despite the Louisiana Science Education Act (which teachers can ignore because its provisions are not mandatory), Louisiana adopted excellent new science standards in 2017, resisting creationist pressure to weaken them (Branch 2017c; Timothy 2017). There are additional reasons for optimism.

Science pedagogy has steadily improved since adoption of the 1960 BSCS curriculum, and the development of more recently updated science education standards portends even further improvements. As of May 2019, the *Next Generation Science Standards*, developed by the National Research Council, the National Science Teaching Association (NSTA), the American Association for the Advancement of Science, and Achieve (a bipartisan group of governors and business organizations), have been adopted by 20 states and the District of Columbia, which comprise 41% of American students (NSTA, n.d.).

The relevant demographics in the United States indicate that the temper of the country is changing in ways that bode well for science education (see Chapters 5 and 12 for additional discussion). Evolution is accepted by almost all religious groups. The majority of denominations—including mainstream Protestant, Catholic, and Jewish groups—support teaching evolution (National Center for Science Education 2008). According to one recent Gallup poll, support for creationism is at its lowest point in 35 years, with only 38% of Americans saying that God created humans in their present form within the last 10,000 years (Swift 2017). The population of white evangelical Protestants, the most important support base for creationism, is declining (Jones and Cox 2017), while the religiously unaffiliated population is expanding rapidly (Pew Research Center 2015a). Moreover, most unaffiliated Americans are young and supportive of evolution, with 73% of those ages

18–29 accepting it (Pew Research Center 2015b). More generally, the decline in religious affiliation is coupled with more progressive stances on social and political issues such as same-sex marriage, a trend that includes acceptance of evolution by almost two-thirds of the general population (Pew Research Center 2015c).

LESSONS AND CAVEATS

The persistent creationist resistance to teaching evolution can be discouraging to teachers and pro-science activists. Although their influence is waning, creationists *never* give up and go away. In addition, creationist organizations are well funded. The total annual revenue of each of the three major creationist organizations dwarfs that of the National Center for Science Education (which was $1,076,055 in 2015): the Institute for Creation Research, $12,344,544 in 2016; Answers in Genesis, which built the infamous Creation Museum, $22,530,213 in 2016; and the Discovery Institute, $5,928,826 in 2015 (Charity Navigator 2017). Consequently, it makes good sense to remain prepared to actively defend science education. One example of the need for constant preparedness is a 2017 Florida law that enables any resident of any county to contest specific educational materials, with evolution and climate change being the primary targets of the bill's supporters (Branch 2017b). However, teachers should not let the immediacy and urgency of problems caused by such resistance obscure the progress that has been made. Teachers' primary responsibility is to teach science accurately, regardless of the way cultural winds are blowing.

Taking a historical view can be valuable to teachers in maintaining both a sense of optimism and the steadfastness needed for what will admittedly be a long process of national maturation concerning the areas of science that arouse cultural controversy. Although creationists' shifting tactics and doggedness tend to overshadow the consistent success in defending evolution, the historical trajectory is one of progress toward better science education. The lesson of this trajectory is that all of the relevant factors—the science, the Constitution, and now demographics—are on the side of science teachers, who are the first and best line of defense against creationism.

REFERENCES

Aguillard v. Treen, 440 So. 2d 704 (1983).

Arkansas Act 590. 1981. General Acts, 73rd General Assembly, State of Arkansas. *Science, Technology, Human Values* 7 (40): 11–13.

Bennetta, W. J. 1988. The rise and fall of the Louisiana creationism law. *Terra* 27 (1): 16–23. *www.ncse. com/library-resource/rise-fall-louisiana-creationism-law.*

Berkman, M., B., and E. Plutzer. 2011. Defeating creationism in the courtroom, but not in the classroom. *Science* 331 (6016): 404–405.

Branch, G. 2012. "Monkey bill" enacted in Tennessee. National Center for Science Education, April 10. *https://ncse.com/news/2012/04/monkey-bill-enacted-tennessee-007299.*

Branch, G. 2017a. Antiscience legislation dies in Texas. National Center for Science Education, May 8. *https://ncse.com/news/2017/05/antiscience-legislation-dies-texas-0018533.*

Branch, G. 2017b. Florida's antiscience bill becomes law. National Center for Science Education, June 28. *https://ncse.com/news/2017/06/floridas-antiscience-bill-becomes-law-0018567.*

Branch, G. 2017c. New science standards in Louisiana. National Center for Science Education, March 8. *https://ncse.com/news/2017/03/new-science-standards-louisiana-0018485.*

Branch, G. 2017d. Victory in Texas. National Center for Science Education, April 21. *https://ncse.com/news/2017/04/victory-texas-0018518.*

Branch, G. 2018. William J. Bennetta dies. National Center for Science Education, October 9. *https://ncse.com/news/2018/10/william-j-bennetta-dies-0018808.*

Charity Navigator. 2017. *www.charitynavigator.org.*

Discovery Institute. n.d. Model Academic Freedom Bill. *www.academicfreedompetition.com/freedom.php.*

Edwards v. Aguillard, 482 U.S. 578 (1987).

Epperson v. Arkansas, 393 U.S. 97 (1968).

Forrest, B. 1997. Combating creationism in a Louisiana school system. *Textbook Letter*, July–August. *www.noanswersingenesis.org.au/combatingcreationismforrest.htm.*

Forrest, B. 2008. Still creationism after all these years: Understanding and counteracting intelligent design. *Integrative and Comparative Biology* 48 (2): 189–201.

Forrest, B. 2010. It's déjà vu all over again: The intelligent design movement's recycling of creationist strategies. *Evolution: Education and Outreach* 3 (2): 170–182.

Forrest, B., and P. R. Gross. 2007. *Creationism's Trojan horse: The wedge of intelligent design.* New York: Oxford University Press.

Green, J. 2004. The Jesus factor: Interview with John Green. *Frontline*, April 29. Public Broadcasting System. *www.pbs.org/wgbh/pages/frontline/shows/jesus/interviews/green.html.*

Hargrove, B. 2013. Creationists' last stand at the State Board of Education. *Dallas Observer*, November 14. *www.dallasobserver.com/news/creationists-last-stand-at-the-state-board-of-education-6431134.*

Jones, R. P., and D. Cox. 2017. *America's changing religious identity: Findings from the 2016 American Values Atlas.* Washington, DC: Public Religion Research Institute. *www.prri.org/wp-content/uploads/2017/09/PRRI-Religion-Report.pdf.*

Kitzmiller et al. v. Dover Area School District, 400 F. Supp. 2d 707 (M.D. Pa. 2005).

Ledbetter, C. 1979. The antievolution law: Church and state in Arkansas. *Arkansas Historical Quarterly* 38 (4): 299–327.

Levitan, D. *Time.* 2017. Donald Trump's science denial is becoming national policy. January 25.

Louisiana Act 473. 2008. Louisiana Science Education Act. Louisiana State Legislature, Regular Session.

Louisiana Senate Bill No. 86 (Act No. 685). 1981. Louisiana Revised Statutes.

McLean Documentation Project. 2005. Complaint, May 27, 1981. U.S. District Court, Eastern District of Arkansas, Western Division.

McLean v. Arkansas Board of Education, 529 F. Supp. 1255 (E.D. Ark. 1982).

McVicar, M. J. 2016. The Religious Right in America. *Oxford Research Encyclopedias.* doi: 10.1093/ acrefore/9780199340378.013.97.

Montgomery, P. 2017. The Religious Right moves to cement political power under Trump. *American Prospect*, September 1. *http://prospect.org/article/religious-right-moves-cement-political-power-under-president-trump.*

Moore, R. 2002. *Evolution in the courtroom: A reference guide.* Santa Barbara, CA: ABC-CLIO.

National Center for Science Education (NCSE). 2008. Religious organizations. In *Voices for evolution*, ed. C. Sager, 98. Berkeley, CA: NCSE. *https://ncse.com/files/Voices_3e%5B1%5D.pdf.*

National Center for Science Education (NCSE). 2009. Discovery Institute's "Model Academic Freedom Statute on Evolution." *https://ncse.com/node/11929.*

National Science Teaching Association (NSTA). n.d. About the *Next Generation Science Standards. http://ngss.nsta.org/about.aspx* (accessed May 25, 2019).

Numbers, R. L. 1982. Creationism in 20th-century America. *Science* 218 (4572): 538–544.

Pew Research Center. 2015a. *America's changing religious landscape.* May 12. *http://assets.pewresearch. org/wp-content/uploads/sites/11/2015/05/RLS-08-26-full-report.pdf.*

Pew Research Center. 2015b. *Americans, politics and science issues.* July 1. *http://assets.pewresearch.org/ wp-content/uploads/sites/14/2015/07/2015-07-01_science-and-politics_FINAL-1.pdf.*

Pew Research Center. 2015c. Social and political attitudes. In *U.S. public becoming less religious*, November 3, 97. *http://assets.pewresearch.org/wp-content/uploads/sites/11/2015/11/201.11.03_RLS_II_ full_report.pdf.*

Scott, E. 2009. *Evolution vs. creationism: An introduction. 2nd ed.* Westport, CT: Greenwood Press.

Swift, A. *Gallup News.* 2017. In U.S., belief in creationist view of humans at new low. May 22. *http:// news.gallup.com/poll/210956/belief-creationist-view-humans-new-low.aspx.*

Tammy Kitzmiller et al. v. Dover Area School District. 2004. Complaint, December 14. U.S. District Court, Middle District of Pennsylvania. *www.aclupa.org/download_file/view_inline/181/294.*

Thompson, H. 2012. *Nature.* Tennessee 'monkey bill' becomes law. April 11. *www.nature.com/news/ tennessee-monkey-bill-becomes-law-1.10423.*

Timothy, P. 2017. Committee denies LC's Warren's edits for state's new science standards. *Baptist Message*, February 14. *http://baptistmessage.com/committee-denies-lcs-warrens-edits-states-new-science-standards.*

Can You Teach *That* in a Science Class? The Legality of Addressing Religious Beliefs During Science Instruction in Public Schools

Ronald S. Hermann

Not long ago, I was invited to give a presentation on the legality of addressing religion during evolution instruction in public schools. Among those in the audience were the concerned parents of a middle school student whose science teacher was clearly not teaching within the confines of the law. It was well known among the students and community that the teacher maintained strong religious beliefs and that those beliefs influenced his teaching. For example, he would not acknowledge the approximately 4.6 billion-year-old age of the Earth and he stated that dinosaurs and humans walked the Earth together.

Frustrated by the teacher's resistance to change his approach, the parents met with school and district administrators and were disturbed by the lack of seriousness about addressing the issue. The parents invited the teacher and administrators to my presentation. So, I set out to address all aspects of the issue in a fair and sensitive manner while framing the legal constraints of addressing science and religion in a public school classroom in an up-front manner. Much of what I presented and the discussion that ensued forms the basis of this chapter. Although my emphasis is on evolution, the lessons are easily extended to other domains of science with potential religious implications for students.

WE ARE TEACHERS OF SCIENCE, NOT LAWYERS

If you are reading this, chances are you are a teacher of science and not a lawyer. My exploration into the topic began when I was teaching science in a public school in Maryland. I was invited to a colleague's language arts class where her students were discussing the play *Inherit the Wind*. I was working on my doctorate at the time; my colleague knew that my research (Hermann 2008) was on the teaching and learning of evolution, and so she invited me to the class to serve as an expert on the matter. I sat in on the class during my planning period and participated in one of the most memorable and robust discussions about science and religion that I have had. For years, I had been teaching the science of evolution, but I had always felt like I never really had the precious class time required to discuss evolution in the larger context of its historical and social implications. In a language arts class, however, I had the freedom and expectation to not focus solely on the science. Instead, we discussed why evolution is science and why creationism and intelligent design are not science.

The students had comments and questions about the validity of evolution, eugenics, Darwin's ideas and misunderstandings, and the Scopes trial. It was a discussion that generally would not take place in a science classroom where the emphasis is likely on content standards. However, I felt the discussion was a positive experience for everyone in the room, even for those students who were reluctant to learn about, or accept, evolution. Such discussions are, in my opinion, necessary for science classrooms and can be done in a respectful, legal manner.

THE NEED FOR A LEGAL FRAMEWORK

Around the same time that I sat in on the class, I was working on an article about why evolution is a socioscientific issue and different classroom methods for responsibly teaching it. In brief, socioscientific issues are those aspects of science that intersect with other ways of knowing about the world such as economics, politics, religion, and philosophy. One way to approach such issues in the classroom is to have students share what they know about the different ways people, or groups of people, respond to a particular science concept. In the case of evolution, this invariably leads to the perspectives of different religious groups. This work led me to many discussions with science teachers and science teacher educators about the teaching of evolution in public school settings. These discussions often resulted in questions and comments about the extent to which religion can be discussed within the confines of the law. Most of us are well informed about attempts to introduce religion into the science classroom to, for example, present nonscientific alternatives to evolution (see Chapter 3 for a more comprehensive overview). But, what about the idea of introducing religion into the science classroom to enhance evolution instruction and to make distinctions between what is and what is not science? As it turns out, many of the people I discussed this topic with were either unsure that religion could be introduced in science classrooms or adamant that it cannot under any circumstance be introduced within the confines of the law.

I presented at a regional National Science Teaching Association conference and the feedback from the teachers, both in their body language and their questions, made it fairly clear that many are not comfortable with the idea of introducing religion into the science classroom for any reason. Later, I presented similar ideas at conferences for science teacher educators, mostly university professors who teach classes in preservice and inservice science teacher education. After one of my presentations, a colleague said something to the effect of "discussing religion in a science class is not something science teachers can legally do, but it may be OK for another class like social studies or language arts." It was at that moment I fully realized that in addition to the possibility that K–12 science teachers are not fully aware of the legal parameters of teaching evolution, science educators responsible for training those teachers may not be aware of the legal implications as well.

So, I conducted a small survey to determine the extent to which science teachers were informed about legal cases related to the teaching of evolution in public schools. I conducted a literature search, and wouldn't you know it, someone had already done the study! In 2004, Randy Moore found that 27% of 103 biology teachers in Minnesota believed they had the choice to teach creationism in the science curriculum. Further, 29% of the teachers thought it was still a crime to teach evolution in some parts of the United States. Knowing this study had already been conducted, I turned my focus to informing science teachers and science teacher educators about the legal aspects of teaching evolution and other intersections of science and religion in public schools.

The remainder of this chapter covers four approaches you will want to consider and the legal implications for each. These approaches range from procedural neutrality, which is both effective in the classroom and legal, to advocating religion, which is ineffective and illegal. Further, I provide you with some examples of what each approach might look like in your science classroom. As you reflect on your own teaching practice and ponder changes to that practice, it is important to discuss those changes with administrators and seek legal counsel to ensure that your approach is supported by school and district administrators and is within the confines of the law.

PROCEDURAL NEUTRALITY

My research on the teaching and learning of evolution has always been conducted in such a way as to consider what it would be like for a student in a science class learning about evolution but maintaining ideas that run counter to science. What would this student who does not believe in evolution—who thinks that believing in evolution is an affront to his or her religion—want to hear and experience? Some science teachers ask their students to share their understandings of evolution, including the perspectives of various religions and religious groups. This approach is called procedural neutrality. But often, the science teachers and science teacher educators I speak with believe that this approach cannot be enacted legally in public school science classrooms. That, however, is not the case.

There is a legal test written by the U.S. Supreme Court, the Lemon test, that you can use as a guideline to determine whether your classroom actions might violate the Establishment Clause of the First Amendment. In *Lemon v. Kurtzman* (1971), the Supreme Court developed the test that includes three prongs: (1) the act must have a bona fide secular purpose, (2) the act's principal or primary effect must be one that neither advances nor inhibits religion, and (3) the act must not result in an excessive entanglement of government with religion (Lofaso 2009). As long as your science instruction has a secular purpose (e.g., teaching evolution as science), does not advocate for a specific religion or demean other religions, and does not excessively address religion when the content topic is scientific, you can legally engage students in discussions of the differences between science and religion. A procedural neutrality approach can be effective at reducing feelings of alienation among students who are resistant to evolution or other concepts and have ideas that run counter to established scientific explanations.

Teachers I have spoken with sometimes question this approach. I can understand the position that evolution is no different from any other topic that science teachers are charged with teaching, along with the disdain some teachers have for the idea that they need to address evolution differently from other topics such as cell theory, plant physiology, and human body systems. From a socioscientific standpoint, however, evolution is different and warrants additional time given the frequent social nature of the controversy. Students may come to appreciate how they can maintain religious beliefs while developing a stronger understanding of the scientific evidence for evolution.

There is emerging evidence that the time spent discussing the interaction of science and religion may positively affect students' views. In one case, an Arizona State University instructor spent two weeks exploring students' religious beliefs during lessons on the development and diversification of life. The number of college students perceiving a conflict between religion and evolution at the start of instruction was cut in half by the end (Barnes, Elser, and Brownell 2017). In a follow-up study, researchers found that as little as six minutes of instruction illustrating the compatibility of religion and evolution resulted in some students reducing their level of perceived conflict (Truong, Barnes, and Brownell 2018). The researchers identified eight distinct aspects of instruction that students stated reduced their perceived conflict, including instructors who are respectful of students with multiple viewpoints on evolution. Another study concluded that high school students are capable of becoming more accepting of evolution when instruction is focused on understanding the supporting evidence and ways of relating evolution and religious beliefs, but not on changing their religious beliefs (Yasri and Mancy 2016).

One of the editors of this book, Lee Meadows, wrote a book in 2009 entitled *The Missing Link: An Inquiry Approach for Teaching All Students About Evolution* (see Chapter 7), which provides examples for how teachers can engage all students, and resistant students in particular, in learning about evolution. Interested readers are encouraged to carefully read *The Missing Link*, discuss the approaches described in the book with administrators, and give additional thought to how ideas in the book can be implemented in the classroom. The following are some suggestions from the book:

- Ask students why people need to know about evolution to understand current events.

- Show a video of someone challenging the validity of evolution, and ask if the views of people the students know may be represented by the person in the video.

- Ask students to pair up and brainstorm concerns they may have about studying evolution.

- Ask students to anonymously write individual concerns on index cards or to write that they do not have any concerns and what they hope to get out of studying evolution.

- Ask students to have a small-group discussion about why they cannot just skip evolution in class and then report their conclusions to the whole class.

I realize that not all teachers of science will feel comfortable with the procedural neutrality approach, for a variety of reasons. Some may feel that they don't possess a broad enough knowledge of different religions or of the similarities and differences of those belief systems. Others may not feel comfortable asking students to share the views of different religions because the conversation may go in a direction they want to avoid. However, here too, the law protects you. If students' expressions are disruptive to your class and will interfere with the schoolwork or discipline of other students, those expressions can be suppressed. Teachers must tolerate students' personal expressions, though they may regulate speech that "disrupts classwork or involves substantial disorder or invasion of the rights of others" (*Tinker v. Des Moines Independent Community School District* 1969). Additionally, you can regulate student speech even in the absence of a significant disruption if there are legitimate pedagogical concerns (*Hazelwood School District v. Kulmeier* 1988); you could end discussions if students advocate for a particular religion or demean other religions. You also have the right to guide the discussion away from anti-science statements. Ultimately, the sole purpose for introducing religion into the science classroom is to help all students come to understand science, the nature of science, and the practices of science without fear that their religious beliefs must be altered to do so.

AFFIRMATIVE NEUTRALITY

Affirmative neutrality is an approach for addressing socioscientific issues in which the teacher provides multiple vantage points to the students. By providing the information yourself, you can filter what is presented, determine the amount of time devoted to the discussion, and guide the amount and nature of student engagement in the discussion. You must provide a neutral approach when discussing, for example, the creation stories of various religions. Again, the Lemon test is applicable in determining whether instruction falls within the legal parameters. The Lemon test was clarified to ask whether the purpose is to convey a message of endorsement or disapproval of religion (*Lynch v. Donnelly* 1984). The Supreme Court "approvingly discussed the idea that public schools can instruct students on the role that religion has played in history and its role in historical controversies so long as the school does not teach religious dogma as true or attempt to inculcate religious values" (Lofaso 2009, p. 79).

Students who are resistant to learning about evolution may be interested to hear about the Clergy Letter Project (*www.theclergyletterproject.org*), which was designed to demonstrate that religion and science can be compatible and to elevate the quality of the dialogue. More than 14,000 clergy have signed letters stating that science and religion are complementary and that the science of evolution need not be in conflict with personal religious beliefs. Similarly, students may be interested in the book *Voices for Evolution* (Sager 2008), in which numerous scientific, religious, and educational organizations developed position statements supporting the teaching of evolution (see Chapter 2 for additional resources).

There is reason to believe that some students want to hear why religious explanations are not considered valid in a scientific framework. Donnelly, Kazempour, and Amirshokoohi (2009) reported that the high school students they interviewed suggested that religious explanations should be included in science instruction. They also reported that some of the evolution rejecters were able to learn evolution by justifying it as one possible perspective. That is to say, some students learned scientific explanations as a way of understanding evolution distinct from other perspectives, including religious ones. Reiss (2010, p. 97) suggested, "Teaching about aspects of religion in science classes could potentially help students better understand the strengths and limitations of the ways in which science is undertaken, the nature of truth claims in science, and the importance of social contexts for science." After all, if students do not understand these aspects upon entering your classroom and you do not teach them in your classroom, then when will the students come to understand these ideas?

Affirmative neutrality is a more teacher-centered approach than procedural neutrality, which can help you ensure that instruction stays within the parameters of the law. It is critically important that you present multiple views and discuss differences between science and non-science without the perception that you are doing so to advance a particular religion. If you do have a particular religious view, you must ensure it is not communicated to students to a greater or lesser extent than other views. If you employ this approach, you must do so in order to teach to those students who may be reluctant to learn about science, perhaps evolution in particular, because of their religious beliefs. Instructional time devoted to science content must clearly outweigh the time devoted to different, especially religious, views.

ADVOCACY

As you surely have experienced, when it comes to the interaction between science and religion, there are some very passionate people on all parts of the continuum. Often these people advocate for a particular approach to the teaching of evolution, and the same is true for teachers. There are at least two types of advocates, and each type has the potential to alienate some groups of students.

At first glance, there may not seem to be any issues with advocating for evolution as the only scientifically valid explanation for the diversity and proliferation of life on Earth. Certainly, there are no legal issues, and this type of instruction is clearly in compliance with the law. In fact, teachers who are advocates for teaching evolution are likely to thoroughly cover evolution (Trani 2004), which is, indeed, a very good thing. However, some teachers may alienate students who are reluctant to learn about evolution. A teacher I know is a staunch advocate for science and a vocal and dedicated advocate for evolution. This teacher does not permit discussions of religion in the classroom. This teacher has knowingly alienated students who hold religious views that run counter to accepted science. I have heard stories that this teacher may have, on occasion, made statements directly to students that basically suggested their thinking on the matter is inferior, flawed, or flat-out wrong. This teacher believes that if students are presented with evidence and the content coverage in the classroom is well presented and of sufficient duration, the students will come to understand and accept the theory of evolution. Like this teacher, approximately 28% of 926 practicing teachers surveyed in one study would be considered strong advocates for teaching evolution (Berkman and Plutzer 2011). If you advocate for evolution, it is our hope that you will reflect upon your instruction to evaluate the extent to which you may alienate students intentionally or unintentionally.

One aspect to reflect on is the extent to which your students will feel alienated from you, the course content, and possibly their peers as a result of instruction that is abrasively challenging their beliefs. Students perceiving a conflict with their beliefs are often not vocal and internalize the conflict. This can result in disdain or complete withdrawal (Scharmann 1994), both of which can be difficult to detect. In 2012, I interviewed public high school Advanced Placement biology students with sophisticated understandings of evolution, but who did not accept evolution because they felt it ran counter to their religious beliefs (Hermann 2012). The students felt somewhat alienated because their religious beliefs were often ignored or omitted from class discussions. My co-editor Lee (Meadows 2009) cautioned that when students are told they will be sticking to the science and not discussing faith, the students often interpret that as meaning their faith is not important. Thus, when we choose to advocate for evolution and other scientific concepts, we must be cognizant of the manner in which we do so. There is nothing inherently wrong with wanting to provide your students with scientifically valid explanations of the natural world. That is our job, but we should be mindful of how we present that material.

By contrast, some teachers knowingly advocate for nonscientific, often religiously motivated, alternatives to evolution. Berkman and Plutzer (2011) reported that 13% of the 926 practicing teachers surveyed explicitly advocate for teaching creationism or intelligent design with another 5% endorsing alternatives to a lesser extent. Advocates for alternatives include statements that either question the scientific validity of evolution or present creationism or intelligent design as valid science.

This type of instruction is clearly in violation of the law. Teaching intelligent design was found to be unconstitutional by a federal district court in Pennsylvania (*Kitzmiller et al. v. Dover Area School District* 2005). The court concluded that intelligent design is not science because (a) it violates the ground rules of science by invoking and permitting supernatural causation, (b) the central tenet of intelligent design employs a flawed and illogical contrived dualism, and (c) it has been deemed unscientific by the scientific community. While you may disagree with these conclusions, they are the law and failure to adhere to them can result in legal action (see Chapter 3 for a more comprehensive legal history).

But, some might ask, "Don't teachers have academic freedom to teach what they want?" Well, not really. If you are a public school science teacher, you cannot invoke the claim of academic freedom to teach your personal beliefs (*Peloza v. Capistrano Unified School District* 1994). The court concluded that, as a school teacher, you are not an ordinary citizen while in contact with students. As such, you cannot deny the theory of evolution or discuss your personal religious views within a science class. Additionally, you cannot invoke the right of free speech to reference personal religious beliefs while teaching, even if the stated purpose is to help students develop an open mind (*Webster v. New Lenox School District* 1990). Actions that can be perceived as being unconstitutional likely will be found unconstitutional. For example, the court has ruled that simply by keeping a copy of a Bible on your desk during the school day you can be perceived as trying to communicate religious beliefs to students (*Roberts v. Madigan* 1990). Thus, both implicit and explicit messages can be viewed as advocating for a particular religious belief system.

There are instances when teachers teach alternatives to evolution and are not challenged by the legal system. There are communities throughout the United States where such instruction is welcomed and encouraged (Long 2011). In these communities, there may not be anyone willing to bring attention to the fact that the instruction violates the law. However, these school systems are in violation of the law and could be subject to legal challenges, which could have a disastrous effect on the financial well-being of the school system. In *Epperson v. Arkansas* (1968), the U.S. Supreme Court unanimously declared Arkansas's anti-evolution statute prohibiting the teaching of evolution as unconstitutional because it violated the Establishment Clause. Laws mandating that time be spent teaching alternatives to evolution alongside evolution have also been found to violate the Establishment Clause (e.g., *Edwards v. Aguillard* 1987). The settlement for *Kitzmiller et al. v. Dover Area School District* (2005; discussed in Chapters 2 and 3) was $1,000,011 in legal fees and damages to the parents and their lawyers. Richard Katskee, assistant legal director for Americans United for Separation of Church and State, noted that "any board thinking of trying to do what the Dover board did is going to have to look for a bill in excess of $2 million" (National Center for Science Education 2006).

If you are in a situation where you are encouraged by school district administrators to teach alternatives to evolution, simply stating that evolution is science and alternatives to evolution are not may not provide a compelling argument to dissuade those administrators. However, informing them of the very real, and severe, financial implications of teaching alternatives to evolution may help them more fully appreciate the severity of the issue. Yes, it would be great if administrators supported the teaching of evolution solely because it is valid science and alternatives are not, but if that argument falls on deaf ears, then informing the administrators of a potential $2 million penalty for not adhering to the law may help them understand the consequences.

AVOIDANCE

One natural response to teaching socioscientific issues such as evolution is to avoid the issue altogether. For some teachers, avoiding topics that are controversial, or that are at least viewed as socioscientific controversies, seems to provide a way to remove themselves from addressing the interaction of science and religion. In the previously referenced survey, 60% of the 926 teachers are not strong advocates for evolution, or its alternatives, to avoid controversy (Berkman and Plutzer 2011). Just how many teachers completely avoid evolution is not clear. Rutledge and Mitchell (2002) found that between 23% and 45% of the 552 Indiana public high school biology teachers they surveyed reported that they avoid or briefly mention evolution in their biology classroom. Among Canadian preservice elementary school teachers, almost a third had reservations about teaching evolution or planned to avoid it entirely (Asghar, Wiles, and Alters 2007).

Teachers may avoid teaching the topic of evolution for several different reasons. Some teachers have creationist views or believe intelligent design to be valid science, so they choose not to teach about the origin of life or differentiation of species over time. Some teachers just do not want to have to worry about offending students or their parents, or in some cases they are pressured to teach alternatives to evolution by members of the community. Untenured teachers may avoid teaching evolution to avoid controversy, and in some locations they may experience, or perceive, pressure to teach alternatives. Other teachers do not feel prepared to discuss the interaction between science and religion in the classroom because of their insufficient knowledge about different religions.

There is nothing inherently illegal about avoiding certain topics as long as you do not make explicit statements that you are doing so because of your religious beliefs. In the case of evolution, however, the topic is valid science and an integral part of the science curriculum. Teachers who avoid teaching evolution are consciously choosing to omit substantial portions of the science curriculum, which is often based on state or national standards. Evolution undergirds much of science across domains ranging from anatomy to zoology. In the eyes of many school districts and state education agencies, avoiding evolution is viewed as poor teaching, and teachers who do so are considered to be derelict in their duties. Choosing to avoid teaching portions of the science curriculum may be grounds for termination. If you avoid teaching evolution, your school district can require you to teach it (*Peloza v. Capistrano Unified School District* 1994). As this book lays out, knowing the different ways in which teachers can approach teaching controversial issues such as evolution will help those of you currently avoiding evolution instruction to reconceptualize what instruction could look like in your classroom.

TEACHING EVOLUTION AND THE LAW

Vaughn and Robbins (2017) provide some strategies for teaching about evolution and the law that have implications for students' attitudes toward and understanding of evolution. Although their work was done with preservice teachers, the activities can be implemented with little modification for public school students. They required students to write a three- to five-page paper about the legal and philosophical basis of teaching evolution in public school classrooms. Students read Supreme Court decisions (*Epperson v. Arkansas* 1968; *McLean v. Arkansas Board of Education* 1982; *Edwards v. Aguillard* 1987; *Peloza v. Capistrano Unified School District* 1994; *Kitzmiller et al. v. Dover Area School District* 2005) and other readings from books, magazines, peer-reviewed papers, and more. The students also read statements from religious organizations endorsing evolution (see Sager 2008) and from religious scientists discussing how they reconcile their beliefs.

> *"As you consider your current approach to teaching topics at the intersection of science and religion, we hope you consider both the legal parameters and the extent to which you can engage all students, even those with some anti-science views, in learning science."*

Perhaps the most challenging activity to replicate would be to provide guest lecturers from theology and philosophy. These lectures were designed to speak about the different benefits and purposes of myth, science, truth, and fact. Vaughn and Robbins (2017) found that when the preservice teachers were required to read and write about Supreme Court cases, their opinions shifted significantly. Support for teaching intelligent design and creationism declined from 26% to 11.5%. The authors indicate that only when assigned a paper including reading and analysis of specific courtroom challenges did a large majority of students support teaching evolution. At the very least, their work suggests that having students read relevant Supreme Court decisions is a useful tool for them to learn about the philosophy of science.

SUMMARY

The parents of the middle school student described at the beginning of this chapter expressed the challenges and responsibilities that lie ahead of us. Their story, while disturbing, illustrates that there are knowledgeable parents who are aware of what is, and is not, being taught in their children's science classrooms. Their child's teacher was clearly not within the parameters of the law and the parents took appropriate action to remove their child from the class. As you consider the extent to which your own teaching adheres to established legal parameters, also consider the teaching of your peers, both in your school and in your school system. It is yet to be seen if, as in other cases cited in this chapter and in Chapter 3, legal action will be taken against the teacher, school, and school district.

As you consider your current approach to teaching topics at the intersection of science and religion, the authors of this book hope you'll consider both the legal parameters and the extent to which you can engage all students, even those with some anti-science views, in learning science. Some approaches may be well within the legal parameters but can isolate or alienate students with different views. Other approaches are clearly outside the law but may be consistent with what some students want to hear. In addition to making instructional decisions at the level of individual, daily lessons, we strongly urge you to take the time to consider the legality of your overarching approach to addressing science and religion issues in your public school classroom.

While the topic of discussing the relationship between science and religion may have you feeling anxious when considering the legality of doing so, we do not want you to worry. Through my exploration into the legality of introducing religious ideas in public schools, I have learned that not only is it possible to legally do so, but it may be beneficial to do so to engage students who are reluctant to learn about science due to their religious beliefs. The law is clear on what can and cannot be done, and we hope that this chapter leaves you more confident in addressing science and religion in your classroom so you can provide a supportive and nonthreatening environment for learning science.

REFERENCES

Asghar, A., J. R. Wiles, and B. Alters. 2007. Canadian pre-service elementary teachers' conceptions of biological evolution and evolution education. *McGill Journal of Education* 42 (2): 189–208.

Barnes, M. E., J. Elser, and S. E. Brownell. 2017. Impact of a short evolution module on students' perceived conflict between religion and evolution. *American Biology Teacher* 79 (2): 104–111.

Berkman, M. B., and E. Plutzer. 2011. Defeating creationism in the courtroom, but not in the classroom. *Science* 331 (6016): 404–405.

Donnelly, L. A., M. Kazempour, and A. Amirshokoohi. 2009. High school students' perceptions of evolution instruction: Acceptance and evolution learning experiences. *Research in Science Education* 39 (5): 643–660.

Edwards v. Aguillard, 482 U.S. 578 (1987).

Epperson v. Arkansas, 393 U.S. 97 (1968).

Hazelwood School District v. Kulmeier, 484 U.S. 260, 271 (1988).

Hermann, R. S. 2008. Evolution as a controversial issue: A review of instructional approaches. *Science & Education* 17 (8–9): 1011–1032.

Hermann, R. S. 2012. Cognitive apartheid: On the manner in which high school students understand evolution without believing in evolution. *Evolution: Education and Outreach* 5 (4): 619–628.

Kitzmiller et al. v. Dover Area School District, 400 F. Supp. 2d 707 (M.D. Pa. 2005).

Lemon v. Kurtzman, 403 U.S. 602 (1971).

Lofaso, A. M. 2009. *Religion in the public schools: A road map for avoiding lawsuits and respecting parents' legal rights*. Washington, DC: Americans United for Separation of Church and State.

Long, D. E. 2011. *Evolution and religion in American education: An ethnography*. Dordrecht, Netherlands: Springer.

Lynch v. Donnelly, 465 U.S. 668 (1984).

McLean v. Arkansas Board of Education, 529 F. Supp. 1255 (E.D. Ark. 1982).

Meadows, L. 2009. *The missing link: An inquiry approach for teaching all students about evolution*. Portsmouth, NH: Heinemann.

Moore, R. 2004. How well do biology teachers understand the legal issues associated with the teaching of evolution? *Bioscience* 54: 860–865.

National Center for Science Education. 2006. "Intelligent design" costs Dover over $1,000,000. *https://ncse.com/news/2006/02/intelligent-design-costs-dover-over-1000000-00899.*

Peloza v. Capistrano Unified School District, 37 F.3d 517 (9th Cir. 1994).

Reiss, M. 2010. Science and religion: Implications for science educators. *Cultural Studies in Science Education* 5 (1): 91–101.

Roberts v. Madigan, 702 F. Supp. 1505, 1513 (D. Colo.1989), *aff'd*, 921 F.2d 1047 (10th Cir. 1990).

Rutledge, M. L., and M. A. Mitchell. 2002. High school biology teachers' knowledge structure, acceptance and teaching of evolution. *American Biology Teacher* 64 (1): 21–28.

Sager, C., ed. 2008. *Voices for evolution*. Berkley, CA: National Center for Science Education.

Scharmann, L. C. 1994. Teaching evolution: The influence of peer teachers' instructional modeling. *Journal of Science Teacher Education* 5 (2): 66–76.

Tinker v. Des Moines Independent Community School District, 393 U.S. 503 (1969).

Trani, R. 2004. I won't teach evolution; it's against my religion: And now for the rest of the story. *American Biology Teacher* 66 (6): 419–427.

Truong, J. M., M. E. Barnes, and S. E. Brownell. 2018. Can six minutes of culturally competent evolution education reduce students' level of perceived conflict between evolution and religion? *American Biology Teacher* 80 (2): 106–115.

Vaughn, A. R., and J. R. Robbins. 2017. Preparing preservice K–8 teachers for the public school: Improving evolution attitudes, misconceptions, and legal confusion. *Journal of College Science Teaching* 47 (2): 7–15.

Webster v. New Lenox School District, 917 F.2d 1004 (7th Cir. 1990).

Yasri, P., and R. Mancy. 2016. Student positions on the relationship between evolution and creation: What kinds of changes occur and for what reasons? *Journal of Research in Science Teaching* 53 (3): 384–399.

What the Public Thinks: Understanding the Current Context for Teaching Scientific Topics With Religious Implications

Kathleen (Casey) Oberlin

The public's interest in science often rests on its ability to be useful in people's daily lives. Science and technology (S&T) improves our ability to access evidence-based medicine, live in cleaner environments, and better understand the natural world around us. A recent National Science Foundation report of public attitudes and understanding of S&T indicates that the majority of Americans think that S&T provides more benefits than harm for society and that it will create more opportunities for future generations, and in general they are interested in the latest S&T developments (National Center for Science and Engineering Statistics [NCSES] 2016, p. 4).

But for many members of society, both in the past and today, science as an institution is often approached with some skepticism, if not distrust at times, as well. A 2016 NCSES report highlights that Americans' average factual scientific knowledge score is higher than the overall trend over time, but not when it comes to topics such as evolution and human origins:

> *49% of Americans correctly indicated that "human beings, as we know them today, developed from earlier species of animals," and 42% correctly indicated that "the universe began with a big explosion." Both scores are relatively low compared with scores on the other knowledge questions in the survey.* (NCSES 2016, p. 46)

Where does this mismatch stem from, when looking at our knowledge of and interest in S&T compared to our subsequent beliefs? Recent work suggests that, in part, for some community members this seeming disconnect between knowledge and beliefs is rooted in a longstanding perception of science as the quintessential secular institution.[1] In a country

---

1 Indeed, while science has never been irreligious, the goal of secular inquiry has marked the contemporary institution of science since the late 1800s as a result of the active pursuit among scholars intent on disentangling science from its religious roots. (For further historical context and current patterns, see Smith 2003; Ecklund 2010; Ecklund and Long 2011; Ecklund, Park, and Sorrell 2011; and Beit-Hallahmi 2015.)

with deep religious traditions, this view of certain scientific areas of research sometimes stands at odds with many people's cultural and moral compass. This in turn shapes their subsequent beliefs.

As a sociologist, I came to study the interface between science and religion through my research on creationism. I conducted over three years of organizational fieldwork at the Creation Museum in Kentucky built by Answers in Genesis. My forthcoming manuscript based on this work is the first book to situate the Creation Museum in the context of the broader creationist social movement. It is an examination of how the politics of plausibility sometimes occurs in unexpected places such as museums. Discussions about believability and trust are seemingly everywhere in this current political era. My research on the Creation Museum informed the focus of this chapter for providing teachers a broader context of the public's varying attitudes, beliefs, and levels of trust in science and religion. These members of the public are many of the same individuals who form families and send their children to your school.

We often want to know on average what most people think. Social science research is a key means to contextualize our own thoughts and experiences in relation to others living across the United States and around the world. Throughout this chapter, my discussion is informed by social science research documenting how the general public interacts with institutional sources of authority (both scientific and religious) in light of variations in their religious beliefs, knowledge of science, and everyday behaviors or activities.[2] I will end with a focus on what the implications of this body of work suggest for science educators, and why it matters what the public thinks, especially for teachers in public schools.

HOW THE PUBLIC PERCEIVES THE RELATIONSHIP BETWEEN SCIENCE AND RELIGION

Laypeople are ordinary members of the public without specialized training in science and are treated in the social science literature as individuals with a mix of scientific knowledge and religious tradition. After all, even those community members among us who do not participate in religious life or are nonbelievers must still engage with a social world full of believers. In this section, I sketch out how social scientists examine (a) the ways in which laypeople's knowledge, attitudes, and perceptions of science relate to sociodemographic patterns; (b) their views of science's role in social life; (c) their degree of trust in institutions of science; and (d) their perspectives about the extent to which science and its practitioners should inform policy decisions.

No single sociodemographic factor explains the variation in perceptions of science and religion, but it is important to track how social group trends may influence the public's understanding. Recent work suggests that individuals belonging to historically margin-

---

2 Throughout the chapter, I use the phrase *interface between science and religion* as a shorthand to refer to the multiple practices, beliefs, and systems of knowledge that inform how the public thinks about scientific topics with religious implications.

alized gender (women), ethno-racial (non-whites), and socioeconomic (lower income) groups are more often associated with less favorable perceptions of the interaction between science and religion.

To examine these patterns further, O'Brien and Noy (2015) used General Social Survey data, a nationally representative survey sample of adults in the United States that is fielded by the independent research organization NORC based at the University of Chicago. They created three categories to capture how the public varies in its views: traditional, postsecular, and modern. The *traditional* category is how the authors classify people who view religion and science as often in conflict and favor religious explanations. *Postsecular* describes people who acknowledge both the significance of science in contemporary society as well as the impact of religion on individuals, even as religious institutional authority declines across society. Both categories, traditional and postsecular, hold religion in favorable regard compared to the *modern* category, which is when respondents explicitly favor science over religion. The researchers found that women were overrepresented in the traditional and postsecular categories. African Americans and Latinos were more likely to fall into the traditional category than the modern category when compared to whites. And, individuals with lower socioeconomic standing followed a similar pattern, leaving the researchers to conclude that "more marginalized people belong to the traditional category" (O'Brien and Noy 2015, p. 104).

In addition, over time in the United States, typically non-whites, women, and those with lower family incomes have maintained consistently low levels of trust in the institution of science (Gauchat 2012). For instance, when it comes to the role of science in informing public policy, non-white respondents indicated less support (Gauchat 2015). Interestingly, however, for the topic of climate change, men are more likely than women to think that scientists do not understand global warming and to want scientists to stay out of public debate involving science.

Living in the southern region of the United States also appears to broadly affect one's view of the interface between religion and science. Longest and Smith (2011) found that emerging adults (approximately 18–23 years old) who lived in the South were more likely to agree with a perspective of *conflict* between science and religion than those living in other regions. O'Brien and Noy (2015) found that those in the postsecular category (acknowledging both science and religion as influential cultural forces) were more likely to live in the South too. And Gauchat (2012) reports that southerners indicated lower levels of trust in science, while Evans and Feng (2013) discovered that both those who live in rural areas nationwide and those who live in the South overall are significantly less likely to believe that scientists understand global warming.

Despite the above findings, generally for many analyses, the influence of sociodemographic factors on individuals' views either declined dramatically or dropped out entirely when researchers considered alternative explanatory factors (Gauchat 2011, 2015; Sherkat

2011). Indeed, some group demographics are associated with particular perceptions of the interplay between religion and science or the extent to which an individual believes in the credibility of scientists and trusts science. Yet the strongest patterns are tied to people's knowledge of science and education, religious tradition (how they identify, what they practice), and political identity. Let's take a closer look at each of these factors.

Education

To assess the public's understanding of science, social scientists examine the general public's command of scientific knowledge in relation to their attitudes about science and technology. Because we tend to have stronger beliefs about issues we perceive as immediately relevant to our daily lives, research typically focuses on areas such as nuclear power sites, medical advancements, genetically modified food, and climate science. In their international meta-analysis, Allum et al. (2008) examined 15 years of scholarship from the early 1990s through the mid-2000s across Europe and North America (40 countries in total). They consistently found stronger evidence of a positive relationship between the general knowledge of science and overall positive attitudes about science across these kinds of topics.

Yet other patterns emerge when education and religious affiliation are taken into account. Sherkat (2011) found that while education level is most strongly associated with scientific literacy, religious affiliation (particularly fundamentalist and sectarian Christianity) is a greater influence than other demographic factors such as gender, race, and income on one's understanding of scientific ideas. Similarly, in an examination of attitudes about evolution, Baker (2013) found that the impact of one's educational attainment hinges on his or her religious belief in biblical literalism. Those who uphold a literal view of the Bible and have high levels of education are more likely to doubt or to not believe in evolution. When O'Brien and Noy (2015) examined trends across their groupings of individuals based upon their perspectives on religion and science, those classified as postsecular had lower levels of education. J. H. Evans (2011) documented that those with lower levels of education have lower levels of scientific knowledge overall, and Sherkat (2011) found a similar pattern between educational level and scientific literacy. Similarly, when comparing those who viewed science and religion as incompatible, Baker (2012) found that those favoring science obtained higher levels of education than those who favored religion.

When exploring the relationship between education and trust in science, the scholarship demonstrates that higher levels of education (measured by years of schooling and highest degree obtained) were associated with greater levels of trust in science (Gauchat 2012). But other factors matter as well. When Scheitle (2011) traced undergraduate students' exposure to more sustained science education (a natural science major/emphasis or not) from their first year in college to their third year, he identified that there was little evidence to support the idea that science education decreases religiosity. Using a nuanced, multifaceted measurement of science, Johnson, Scheitle, and Ecklund (2015) found that religiosity is also not strongly associated with one's interest in or knowledge of science, but it is negatively associated with one's confidence in science (as religiosity increases, confidence decreases).

Religious Tradition

The influence of religious affiliation on one's desire to seek out scientific knowledge is not as prominent as might be expected. J. H. Evans (2011) did not find the anticipated negative relationship between conservative Protestants (including African American Protestants) and the level of scientific knowledge acquired. In effect, a perceived conflict did not restrict them from seeking out information. For instance, when presenting study subjects with a fictional scenario to examine how the participants would wrestle with scientific research due to the moral and ethical concerns the research findings raised, M. S. Evans (2012) unearthed how respondents rarely drew on religious language or reasoning. Those who did raise some concerns did so more in terms of skepticism of modernity rather than a belief in an inherent epistemological incompatibility between scientific explanation and religious justification.

Yet religious practice does appear to affect one's trust in science, as Gauchat (2012) indicated that those who more regularly attended church maintained lower levels of trust in science. Again, religious beliefs frequently matter more than other sociodemographic factors. Those who viewed science and religion as incompatible and favored science were less likely to attend religious services, more likely to see the Bible as "history and legends," and three times more likely to identify as agnostic/atheist (Baker 2012, p. 347). Emerging adults who believe there is only one way to heaven (through Jesus) were more likely to agree that there is a conflict between religion and science (Longest and Smith 2011). Both of these studies reveal that the individuals who identify with the science-religion incompatibility perspective are a small subgroup of the broader population. The majority in both studies did not perceive science and religion to be incompatible or conflicting. Yet it is important to unpack consistent patterns even if they operate on the margins.

Political Identity

The relationship among science, religion, and education is further complicated by political affiliation. Recent work suggests that the effect of one's political ideology is tied to one's knowledge of science. Evans and Feng (2013) argued that the strongest predictor of an individual's belief that "scientists do not understand global warming" is that person's political ideology (conservatives more likely than liberals) and political party identification (Republicans and Independents more likely than Democrats). In studies of general levels of trust in the institution of science or views on how scientists should influence public policy, individuals with lower levels of education and scientific literacy indicate less support for the use of science in informing public policy—confirming the scholarship linking higher levels of knowledge with favorable attitudes toward science.

Interestingly, however, Gauchat (2015) highlighted a dynamic interaction between education and political involvement. Highly educated political conservatives indicated less support for the general use of science to inform public policy. In another study, Gauchat (2012) found that more highly educated political conservatives had higher levels of distrust toward, and were more critical of, science. Yet, overall, this same group had lower levels of distrust for other institutions when compared to other political conservatives with less education. O'Brien and Noy (2015) also found support for this trend. Those characterized by a postsecular perspective (who frequently identify as politically conservative) with high levels of scientific literacy were associated with favorable views of science. The only exceptions were when a scientific theory was perceived to contradict their more conservative religious beliefs, and on related controversial subjects (e.g., the Big Bang and human evolution). These findings parallel Baker's (2013) work, mentioned earlier, which revealed a similarly nuanced relationship between educational attainment and views of the Bible. Those with high levels of education, who also support biblical literalism, are less likely to have a firm belief in evolution and are more likely to support teaching creationism in public schools.

Of course, laypeople's individual political identities must inevitably interact with various sources of institutional authority in public life. Much of the scholarship on laypersons' trust in institutional authority relies on the longitudinal General Social Survey data to determine the extent to which the public has confidence in the people running the central institutions or systems (e.g., politics, science, medicine) that govern much of their lives. Over time (1974–2010), Gauchat (2012) found that declining levels of confidence in the institution of science are similar to drops in levels of trust for political sources of institutional authority. But they are also distinct, as there are bumps in the trust afforded to political institutions, but not science, in the post–President Reagan and Bush eras. Specifically, Gauchat indicated that political conservatives experienced the biggest, most consistent drop in their trust of science throughout the latter half of the 20th century.

For these intellectually engaged individuals who possess high levels of general education and scientific literacy, the institution of science and scientists in particular are the primary targets of their institutional distrust and their desire to restrict its influence on society. This contradicts a purely knowledge-attitudes model, which argues that higher levels of education attainment, and scientific literacy, encourage more trust in the institution of science and a belief in an increased influence of science in public policy. More education does not always translate into more trust in or support of science. And, science teachers can probably easily imagine how children growing up in families expressing such institutional distrust might communicate their family values during lessons about evolution or climate change.

UNDERSTANDING THE PUBLIC'S MULTIFACETED ENGAGEMENT WITH SCIENCE AND RELIGION

Generally, scholarship suggests that multiple sources of authority and belief systems are at work in shaping individuals' attitudes and perceptions. It is not just about scientific knowledge, level of educational attainment, practice of religious tradition, or political affiliation. High levels of scientific literacy are associated only with favorable general attitudes about science, not attitudes about scientists' knowledge of particular socioscientific controversies or their influence on policy issues such as stem cell research or climate change. Gauchat (2012) indicated that the amount of alienation—defined as social isolation and lack of confidence in institutions—matters almost as much as scientific literacy. When accounting for public attitudes about science, it becomes increasingly important also to assess the cultural authority of science in the public sphere. For instance, one study found that the location of scientific activity (university laboratories), the perceptions of how it gets done (systematic methods), and the imagined disposition of its practitioners (scientists as objective) increase the likelihood of the public maintaining favorable general attitudes toward science (Gauchat 2011).

Regardless of the sources of authority, members of the public frequently decouple the distinction between scientists' expertise and scientists' ability to influence policy. Politically, Gauchat (2011) indicated that being conservative correlates negatively with favorable attitudes about scientists' understanding and ability to influence public policy. Gauchat claimed that "the public understands that science provides cultural knowledge and understanding vital to public policy decisions, but that this knowledge should not translate directly into political power" (2011, p. 764). Religiously, while conservative Protestants believe in the veracity of the scientists' claims, they question scientists' ability to address the problem, particularly through policy solutions related to longstanding controversies.

J. H. Evans (2011, p. 721) has argued that for scientific issues that have turned into social issues—for example, global warming and stem cell research—the religious counterclaims hold sway over evangelicals and they have "opposed scientists' moral influence in public discussions." These trends uphold predictions in the literature that religious fundamentalists would question both the expertise of scientists and their ability to intervene in public policy, whereas evangelicals would simply question scientists' ability or the dynamics of their intervention, not necessarily their expertise in and of itself (Evans and Feng 2013). In terms of policy claims, evangelicals may have issues with the perceived moral agenda of scientists, seeing scientists as "moral competitors" in these moments (Evans and Feng 2013, p. 596; see J. H. Evans 2018 for a broader discussion). This stems from a historical precedent of many Protestants viewing themselves as in moral conflict with scientists in the public sphere, most notably over evolution, but increasingly over stem cell research and human cloning as well. Similarly, O'Brien and Noy (2015) indicated that only issues rooted in both scientific and religious sources of authority (abortion, embryonic stem cells) produce distinguishable and disparate attitudes among the public. A desire to restrict the influence of scientists only emerges when the issue is politicized as a conflict between scientific and religious claims of authority.

Ultimately, scientific knowledge and level of education do not operate separately as factors solely determining the public's trust of science-related institutions or topics to the extent previously documented (and more frequently assumed). Instead, research increasingly points to how interactions among these bases of knowledge are vital for determining how individuals may negotiate various sources of authority in the contemporary era. Persistent divergences emerge only when particular issues are portrayed as grounded in a moral debate.

CASE STUDY: THE ROLE OF PUBLIC FIGURES IN COMMUNICATING ABOUT SCIENCE AND RELIGION

Given that knowledge of and familiarity with science has long been understood to influence public perceptions of science, many invested in the institution of science dedicate great effort to popularizing science. As journalism and other communications about science often rely on scientific experts to weigh in, the ability of key leaders to influence public discourse is evident. But few studies empirically examine to what extent these well-known scientists and science enthusiasts have an impact. How effective are public figures in altering cognitive boundaries—assessed in relation to business, politics, and public health efforts—around the relationship between science and religion? In a survey experiment administered in the United States, Scheitle and Ecklund (2015) compared two public figures deeply tied to the institution of science and well known for their positions on science and religion. Francis Collins, a scientist who led the Human Genome Project and is now the director of the National Institutes of Health, is known for his evangelical religious beliefs and his view that science and religion are compatible. Alternatively, Richard Dawkins, an evolutionary biologist who publishes prolifically and participates in public debates, is widely regarded as a popularizer of atheism who vigorously advocates against the idea that science and religion are compatible.

Scheitle and Ecklund first asked participants if they had ever heard of Collins or Dawkins; only those unfamiliar with the scientist about whom they were asked were given a description of the scientist, his credentials, and his view of science and religion. If the participants had heard of their respective scientist, they simply moved onto the next question without receiving any descriptive statement (the experimental treatment). Subsequently, those who were unfamiliar with their respective scientist were asked about whether science and religion were in conflict and if they placed themselves on the science or religion side of the conflict, if science and religion were entirely independent from one another, or if science and religion were in collaboration with one another. In comparing those who received the description of the scientist (either Collins or Dawkins) and those who did not (because they indicated previously that they were familiar with the respective scientist), those who received the Collins treatment were significantly more likely to support a collaborative view of science and religion than those who had not received the Collins treatment. There was no difference for Dawkins.

The authors concluded that perhaps public figures in science with unexpected views change public opinion more than those whose beliefs are perceived as expected. Collins's vocal public religiosity and prominence in science, coupled with his collaborative view of science and religion, is less expected given the long-touted conflict between the two sources of authority. Comparatively, Dawkins's positioning is better known among the general public (more of the general sample had heard of him compared to Collins), but his viewpoint was an expected position for a scientist to take. This confirms trends in science communication studies and other work that focus on public figures' engagement with the public, which suggests that we tend to listen to those whom we perceive as similar to us, or in this case Collins. Given the high levels of religiosity across individuals in the United States, this is less surprising to many of us.

Yet, this finding underscores broader trends among the public that play into the popular assumption that the institution of science is inherently secular and the perception that scientists are overwhelmingly atheistic with a general disregard for religion. Despite historical patterns that suggest otherwise, these perceptions have persisted strongly among the public, and often within the professoriate, throughout the 20th and 21st centuries. Those tied to the institutional authority of science, both natural and social scientists, are in a position of influence. Their ability to intervene in broader national conversations about science and religion is arguably greater than the general public's. Given that many prominent scientists are not antireligious, work such as Scheitle and Ecklund's (2015) could be useful in classroom discussions.

CONCLUSION

I wrap up by briefly highlighting a few broader implications about how the public views the interface between science and religion. The role of political affiliation for influencing one's view of the relationship between science and religion is stronger compared to education or other conventional sociodemographic traits such as race, age, or gender. Why is this the case? The impact of key stakeholder efforts—such as from social movement leaders, political lobbyists, and education reformers—appears to matter more than deep, long-standing perceived epistemological issues, as science and religion are not always in conflict. Science teachers

"Based on current social science research, it is imperative to not ignore or sidestep how science as an institution fits into the broader set of social institutions (e.g., education, politics, and religion) that shape our society."

may need to consider how the political affiliations of parents can influence how students approach the learning of certain subjects.

Where and when certain types of knowledge claims are drawn into debates over authority is what primarily shapes the public's engagement with science and religion. Put another way, polarization stems from how cultural, political, or moral stakeholders frame the issues. Topics such as human origins or climate change are better understood when science educators connect how these issues intersect with their students' other beliefs and ideas in their lives, track who has vested interests in shaping their perceptions, and guide them in exploring what the evidence supports.

Based on current social science research, I argue that it is imperative to not ignore or side-step how science as an institution fits into the broader set of social institutions (e.g., education, politics, and religion) that shape our society. As science educators, explicit conversations about how multiple politicized arguments may be made from the same empirical evidence will present opportunities to show students the importance of better understanding the scientific research itself.[3] These sources of information can be effective tools for humanizing science as an institution that is not always perfect; often the public is unclear or misguided about what to believe or whom to trust. I offer three key recommendations:

- Highlight for students the funding sources of a given study (or documentary film, website, etc.) and how this might relate to the types of questions asked and explored. Is it supported by a research institute, a professional association, private industry, or a government agency? Of course, the source of the funding does not necessarily invalidate the work, but it is useful to highlight and critically examine as an example of how science is a social institution operated by people and fueled by resources.

- Guide students in exploring how the data were collected. What are the strengths and limitations of that method, and how does it relate to the types of findings discussed?

- Help students situate how the findings fit into existing scientific explanations, and guide them in a discussion about how much or little consensus there may be about a given topic.

In our work as science educators, we should use contemporary events and current perceived controversies to show students how so much of our scientific knowledge can

---

3 Unpacking scholarly research is one way to engage students critically. Another way is to use social documentary films as well as public opinion surveys and polls. First, PBS is a great resource that surely many teachers already use. Another excellent example is *Merchants of Doubt* (2014); the film is based on work by historians of science who track how misinformation campaigns are not new, using examples throughout the 20th century from the "health" benefits of tobacco and the "safety" of toxic chemicals to the recent "questions" about climate change. Second, while public opinion surveys and polls vary in quality, a few consistently reliable sources with available data sets to explore with students are the General Social Survey and the Pew Research Center. Finally, recent discussions about misleading information or "fake news" could also be useful in classroom activities (Eldred 2017).

be politicized, or not, and what students can do about it. The first step is talking about the situation and analyzing it together.

ACKNOWLEDGMENT

Portions of this chapter were published elsewhere. Used with kind permission from Springer Nature: Kathleen C. Oberlin, "Science," pages 47–66 in *Handbook of Religion and Society*, edited by David Yamane (Switzerland: Springer International Publishing, 2016).

REFERENCES

Allum, N., P. Sturgis, D. Tabourazi, and I. Brunton-Smith. 2008. Science knowledge and attitudes across cultures: A meta-analysis. *Public Understanding of Science* 17 (1): 35–54.

Baker, J. O. 2012. Public perceptions of incompatibility between "science and religion." *Public Understanding of Science* 21 (3): 340–353.

Baker, J. O. 2013. Acceptance of evolution and support for teaching creationism in public schools: The conditional impact of educational attainment. *Journal for the Scientific Study of Religion* 52 (1): 216–228.

Beit-Hallahmi, B. 2015. Explaining the secularity of academics: Historical questions and psychological findings. *Science, Religion and Culture* 2 (3): 104–119.

Ecklund, E. H. 2010. *Science vs. religion: What scientists really think.* New York: Oxford University Press.

Ecklund, E. H., and E. Long. 2011. Scientists and spirituality. *Sociology of Religion* 72 (3): 253–274.

Ecklund, E. H., J. Z. Park, and K. L. Sorrell. 2011. Scientists negotiate boundaries between religion and science. *Journal for the Scientific Study of Religion* 50 (3): 552–569.

Eldred, S. M. 2017. Fake news: How not to fall for it. *Science News for Students.* doi: *www.sciencenews forstudents.org/article/fake-news-how-not-fall-it.*

Evans, J. H. 2011. Epistemological and moral conflict between religion and science. *Journal for the Scientific Study of Religion* 50 (4): 707–727.

Evans, J. H. 2018. *Morals not knowledge: Recasting the contemporary U.S. conflict between religion and science.* Berkeley, CA: University of California Press.

Evans, J. H., and J. Feng. 2013. Conservative Protestantism and skepticism of scientists studying climate change. *Climatic Change* 121 (4): 595–608.

Evans, M. S. 2012. Supporting science reasons, restrictions, and the role of religion. *Science Communication* 34 (3): 334–362.

Gauchat, G. 2011. The cultural authority of science: Public trust and acceptance of organized science. *Public Understanding of Science* 20 (6): 751–770.

Gauchat, G. 2012. Politicization of science in the public sphere: A study of public trust in the United States, 1974 to 2010. *American Sociological Review* 77 (2): 167–187.

Gauchat, G. 2015. The political context of science in the United States: Public acceptance of evidence-based policy and science funding. *Social Forces* 94 (2): 723–746.

Johnson, D. R., C. P. Scheitle, and E. H. Ecklund. 2015. Individual religiosity and orientation towards science: Reformulating relationships. *Sociological Science* 2: 106–124.

Longest, K. C., and C. Smith. 2011. Conflicting or compatible: Beliefs about religion and science among emerging adults in the United States. *Sociological Forum* 26 (4): 846–869.

National Center for Science and Engineering Statistics (NCSES). 2016. *National Science Board: Science and engineering indicators 2016.* Arlington, VA: National Science Foundation.

O'Brien, T. L., and S. Noy. 2015. Traditional, modern, and post-secular perspectives on science and religion in the United States. *American Sociological Review* 80 (1): 92–115.

Scheitle, C. P. 2011. Religious and spiritual change in college: Assessing the effect of a science education. *Sociology of Education* 84 (2): 122–136.

Scheitle, C. P., and E. H. Ecklund. 2015. The influence of science popularizers on the public's view of religion and science: An experimental assessment. *Public Understanding of Science* 26 (1): 25–39.

Sherkat, D. E. 2011. Religion and scientific literacy in the United States. *Social Science Quarterly* 92 (5): 1134–1150.

Smith, C. 2003. *The secular revolution: Power, interests, and conflict in the secularization of American public life.* Berkeley, CA: University of California Press.

PART II

Practical Suggestions
for All Teachers of Science

Addressing Science-Religion Interactions by Teaching About Science in the Elementary Grades

Ian C. Binns and Mark Bloom

Teaching science can be a challenging endeavor, especially for elementary school teachers. While we recognize that if you are reading this you are probably an elementary teacher with a special interest in science, it is important to know that many elementary teachers are not as comfortable with science. In fact, only 31% of elementary teachers feel very well prepared to teach science, compared to 73% for mathematics and 77% for reading and language arts (Banilower et al. 2018). This is especially true when it comes to teaching topics such as evolution, which many consider controversial. Our research with preservice elementary teachers revealed that more than 50% endorsed the inclusion of creationism or intelligent design in their science curriculum (Binns and Bloom 2017; Bloom and Binns 2018). Teaching such content as genuine science, however, can erode students' perceptions of what is scientifically valid and what is not. Some teachers make this mistake because they, themselves, do not fully know the critical characteristics of a scientific claim. Others understand the distinction between science and non-science, but they err on the side of including the content anyway, out of fear of offending students or parents by passing judgment on a nonscientific idea.

This presents a critically important challenge to evolution education, and science education in general, because the elementary curriculum includes foundational ideas about both science and evolution. To address this challenge, this chapter explores how elementary science standards guide students in distinguishing science from non-science and how they prepare the foundation for later learning about evolution. Additionally, by recognizing these connections and purposefully emphasizing them in the classroom, we can prepare students for future interactions between scientific and religious ideas when, and if, they arise with their peers, families, and teachers.

We believe that students must learn what science is, and how it is a different way of knowing, before they can begin to learn about something as complex as evolution. Several resources are available to help you teach about both science in general and evolution specifically. At the elementary grades, we have found the use of trade books to be helpful. We recommend you start with books that made the Outstanding Science Trade Books for Students K–12 list, an annual awards program sponsored by the National Science Teaching Association and the Children's Book Council. Additionally, two websites that the University of California Museum of Paleontology puts together are useful resources for learning about and teaching science in general ("Understanding Science," *http://undsci.berkeley.edu*) and evolution specifically ("Understanding Evolution," *http://evolution.berkeley.edu*).

Our insights regarding elementary students' knowledge about science come from a number of different sources. Ian has taught elementary science methods courses for more than 10 years and has conducted professional development for inservice elementary teachers. Mark has conducted many years of professional development for inservice science teachers (elementary through high school) and has taught science pedagogy and content courses for preservice elementary teachers. Finally, our research has focused on preservice elementary teachers and their thoughts on teaching evolution, creationism, and intelligent design.

In this chapter, we first define science and identify important characteristics that elementary students should learn about science. Second, we outline concepts that elementary students should learn about evolution. Third, we describe how the identified characteristics about science connect to what elementary students should learn about evolution. Finally, we conclude with implications for elementary science instruction as they relate to our ongoing conversation about science and religion in this book. As with most things in education, it all starts in the elementary grades.

WHAT STUDENTS SHOULD LEARN ABOUT SCIENCE IN ELEMENTARY SCHOOL

The first thing students should learn is what science is in general. As indicated in Chapter 1, the following is a good definition of science: "The use of evidence to construct testable explanations and predictions of natural phenomena, as well as the knowledge generated through this process" (National Academy of Sciences and Institute of Medicine 2008, p. 10). Key concepts in this definition include evidence, testable explanations and predictions, and natural phenomena. Additionally, science involves a diverse community of people. This community supports the idea that science is a collaborative endeavor, must be reproducible, and is subject to peer review.

There are many available resources that address what students should learn about science. We like "Understanding Science" (*http://undsci.berkeley.edu*), an online resource that the University of California Museum of Paleontology has developed. "Understanding Science" provides a conceptual framework outlining what students should learn about a variety of topics, all focused on science, at different grade levels. Elementary school is broken down into two grade bands: K–2 and 3–5. The topics in those two grade bands include the following: (a) What is science? (b) How science works. (c) The social side of science. (d) What has science done for you lately? (e) A scientific approach to life.

We summarize each of those five topics here, noting a few developmental differences between the two grade bands. Note that this is not an exhaustive treatment, but these selected topics are particularly useful to introduce to elementary-age students.

What Is Science?

Three topics in this section from "Understanding Science" help students see the big picture of how science is different from non-science:

- Scientists ask and address questions.

- Scientists base their ideas on evidence from the natural world.

- Scientific ideas may change based on what we observe and experience, and with new evidence.

Scientists ask and address questions. Students need to understand the role of questions in science. Questioning is a fundamental aspect of science, and all scientists ask questions. This is what drives scientific investigation. Questions do not necessarily need to be formal or sophisticated. Scientific questioning can be as simple as observing something in nature and wondering how it happened to be there or how it came to look as it does. Students need to gain experience asking questions as part of the scientific process.

Scientists base their ideas on evidence from the natural world. The first part of this topic—that science requires evidence—is pretty straightforward. As discussed in Chapter 1, there must be verifiable evidence for the scientific community to accept a particular explanation. If this evidence does not exist or cannot be verified by independent scientists, the proposed explanation is discarded. The second part of this topic—that science only addresses the natural world—is the key aspect that distinguishes science from other ways of knowing, such as religion. Science is limited to only answering questions about natural phenomena. Additionally, science can only provide explanations that employ natural processes and cannot invoke supernatural causes.

Scientific ideas may change based on what we observe and experience, and with new evidence. Students need to be provided with experiences that help them understand that current scientific knowledge is subject to change; in other words, science is tentative and nothing in science is absolute. There is always a chance that currently accepted scientific explanations can change based on either the discovery of new evidence or the discovery of new ways to evaluate existing evidence. Too often the word *prove* is used in regards to scientific claims. More accurately, science provides confirming (or disconfirming) evidence to support (or refute) scientific explanations. It is important to characterize the tentativeness of science as a positive attribute; this quality ensures that scientific claims will continue to be refined and improved.

How Science Works

Three topics in this "Understanding Science" section extend the basic principles of science by describing more practical aspects with which you might be familiar through inquiry-based instruction:

- Scientific observations can be made directly with our own senses or indirectly through the use of tools.

- Scientists look for patterns in what they observe.

- Scientists do not always agree with one another.

Scientific observations can be made directly with our own senses or indirectly through the use of tools. Students should be engaged in activities where they come to understand the role and power of observations in science and that we use all five of our senses to make these observations. Elementary students thrive at making lists of observations about phenomena. They should be encouraged to examine things carefully and understand that no observation is too small. Major scientific breakthroughs have occurred because a scientist happened to make a very rare or minute observation (scientist Barbara McClintock's discovery of "jumping genes" provides a good example). Additionally, students should understand that, in many cases, scientists use tools to help make indirect observations and that they make inferences to attempt to explain their observations. Students should be encouraged to make inferences based upon their observations as inferences can lead to questions, predictions, and hypotheses.

Scientists look for patterns in what they observe. Patterns are an important part of science. They help scientists make sense of their observations. Patterns are useful in making predictions, developing explanations, and gaining insights into past events. NASA famously uses the patterns observed about gravity to launch space shuttles and regulate their orbits, and volcanologists use patterns to predict volcanic events. We must provide students with the opportunity to gather and explore data to uncover patterns in what might initially seem to be random or chaotic data.

Scientists do not always agree with one another. Another key aspect to understand is that, in science, scientists do not always agree with one another. Scientists do not spend their careers trying to always support existing knowledge. Scientists work to advance our understandings of all natural phenomena. In many cases, they do not agree with a particular explanation and will go to great efforts to disprove it. Sometimes, disagreements in science can last for long periods of time until enough evidence is collected to finally justify accepting one explanation and discarding its competitor. Until quite recently, for example, scientists disagreed on whether dinosaurs were more like modern-day birds or modern-day reptiles.

Now, the scientific consensus is that dinosaurs were more similar to modern birds. Despite ongoing disagreements within the scientific community, the goal is to develop the best possible explanation based on the available evidence. In other words, students must understand that in science, evidence is key. Without evidence, the scientific community will not accept explanations. Those explanations that withstand such scrutiny persist.

The Social Side of Science

"Understanding Science" next addresses the collaborative and creative sides of science and emphasizes that all people can participate in scientific inquiry. Four topics adapted from this section are essential for students to experience at a young age and throughout their science education:

- Scientists share their ideas and explain their evidence to one another.

- Scientists work together.

- Many different sorts of people do science, and anyone can do science.

- Scientists are creative.

Scientists share their ideas and explain their evidence to one another. In order for any explanation to be accepted by the scientific community, that explanation must be reproducible and undergo a rigorous peer review process. If, using the same parameters, other scientists are unable to reproduce these findings, then the findings are often discarded. Peer checking and accountability directly leads to increased validity, credibility, and confidence in the proposed explanations. Elementary students can be provided with opportunities to peer review the work of their classmates and provide feedback to help clarify, revise, and ultimately strengthen their collective work and understanding. In fact, without giving students the opportunity to emulate the scientific process of revising their work, there is little rationale for providing feedback at all. Students can also share their work through oral presentations and through their writing, both of which are valuable science process skills. Teachers, of course, would need to determine what is developmentally appropriate. For example, K–2 students might not understand the word *evidence* to the extent of grades 3–5 students.

Scientists work together. Science is a collaborative endeavor. The notion that scientists work alone is untrue. Often teams of scientists are led by several individuals. Some scientific articles, for example, can have 20 or more authors. In fact, in recent years, numerous papers in the physical sciences have had more than 1,000 authors! (See Mallapaty 2018.) Each team member has a responsibility and all contributions are valuable to the work. For example, the major advances in climate science today are informed by botanists, mammologists, geologists, oceanographers, and many other specialists. Their specific contributions help climate scientists create models to predict future trends. Chances are your students are already working on projects together, so making this aspect of science explicit may be all that is needed. It is important to let your students know that they are conducting their work in groups just as scientists do.

Many different sorts of people do science, and anyone can do science. We combine two statements from *Understanding Science* here and note that the grades 3–5 version of the first half of this topic states that "the scientific community is diverse," which will make more sense to older students. Students should understand that the scientific community is a diverse community. We argue that all of us are born scientists. Whenever a person is curious about why something happens or asks questions to better understand something, he or she is being scientific. Students should leave elementary school believing that the field of science is open for all people including themselves. Providing students opportunities to learn about scientists beyond those in textbooks is important. Many universities and private companies can provide a range of diverse speakers or field trip opportunities in which students learn about their work so the students can see this diversity firsthand.

Scientists are creative. Science is ultimately a creative endeavor. Scientists use creativity to determine how they will collect evidence in challenging locations such as deep in the oceans or at geothermal vents. Scientists must also use their creative minds to generate inferences to explain observations and to design experiments to test hypotheses. Thomas Edison, for example, famously alluded to the need for creativity in science when he claimed to have discovered 10,000 ways not to make a lightbulb before finally succeeding! Encouraging young students to be creative and do science rather than following prescribed steps can result in creative pursuits that otherwise would not occur.

What Has Science Done for You Lately?

This section from "Understanding Science" includes only one topic, and we believe it is important for students to embrace: People benefit from the knowledge gained through science. Scientific advancements directly affect many aspects of society. A few examples include communication, infrastructure, transportation, medicine, and agriculture. Elementary students can become engaged in this topic simply by examining their classroom environment. Their pencils and pens, lunch containers, projectors, and desks are all examples of materials and technologies that are available thanks to science.

A Scientific Approach to Life

The last topic from "Understanding Science" should resonate with all science educators: Problem solving and decision making benefit from a scientific approach. As we noted earlier, asking questions is a fundamental aspect of the scientific endeavor. Asking questions is also important to solving problems and making decisions that directly benefit us or society. Students can gain experience with this notion with something as ordinary as the formation of condensation on the outside of a glass. For example, students may observe lemonade and ice inside a glass. But after a few minutes, as they pick up the glass, there is water on the table. They might think there is a crack in the glass or they had spilled the lemonade. Upon further inspection, they find no cracks in the glass and realize the liquid is just water. So where did this water come from? These actions depict scientific reasoning with each proposed explanation being tested, discarded, and replaced by another until the solution is found.

WHAT STUDENTS SHOULD LEARN ABOUT EVOLUTION IN ELEMENTARY SCHOOL

As noted throughout this book, understanding basic principles about science helps to avoid common misconceptions about science in general and about topics that might cause serious concerns for some students and teachers. Elementary grades are where we capture students' curiosity and enthusiasm about the natural world and where we introduce scientific concepts that will be extended as students mature. Evolution, we assert, is one of those topics that should be taught throughout a student's education.

Some might declare that evolution is not actually taught in elementary grades. However, after close examination of our professional standards, we identified a number of critical science concepts that build the foundation for understanding and accepting evolution in later grades. Among these concepts are the inheritance of traits, adaptations and natural selection, and geologic time. Each is briefly described here, and you will notice connections to the basic principles of science discussed in the previous section.

Inheritance

As early as first grade, children should begin to learn about heredity and the inheritance of traits. The *Next Generation Science Standards* (*NGSS*), one of our primary professional documents (NGSS Lead States 2013), indicate that first graders should "make observations to construct an evidence-based account that young plants and animals are like, but not exactly like, their parents" (1-LS3-1). By third grade, students should "analyze and interpret data to provide evidence that plants and animals have traits inherited from parents and that variation of these traits exists in a group of similar organisms" (3-LS3-1). Understanding that traits are passed from parent to offspring builds the basis for later learning about Mendelian genetics. Understanding how traits can vary in expression allows for later mastery of the concept that some individuals will be more suited for their environment than others and thus more likely to survive and reproduce—the driving force behind adaptation and natural selection.

Adaptations and Natural Selection

By third grade, the *NGSS* advises that learners should understand that organisms are adapted to their environment and be able to "construct an argument with evidence that in a particular habitat some organisms can survive well, some survive less well, and some cannot survive at all" (3-LS4-3). These same third graders should further understand how the variations within the population affect individual organisms and be able to "use evidence to construct an explanation for how the variations in characteristics among individuals of the same species may provide advantages in surviving, finding mates, and reproducing" (3-LS4-2). These concepts are central to understanding how organisms evolve in response to changing environmental conditions.

Once students have a clear understanding of this content, they can better appreciate the importance of physical characteristics of living things. For example, while they might have previously considered the stripes of a zebra as aesthetically pleasing, they can now look for an explanation behind them, namely to protect zebras from predation by big cats. Similarly, the color patterns of quite different species such as sea turtles and sparrows (think light-colored bellies and dark-colored backs) also protect from predation. Students can understand the advantage of coloration with regards to sexual selection of animals and pollination in plants. Understanding adaptations and natural selection allows elementary students to recognize that the myriad characteristics they observe among living things are not randomly derived, but rather the result of evolutionary forces over many generations.

Geologic Time Scale

The second-grade *NGSS* standards include content regarding the age of planet Earth. Second graders should be able to "use information from several sources to provide evidence that Earth events can occur quickly or slowly" (2-ESS1-1). By third grade, students should be able to understand that some living organisms today look similar to organisms now extinct, which begins to provide evidence for common ancestry. Further, students should be able to "analyze and interpret data from fossils to provide evidence of the organisms and the environments in which they lived long ago" (3-LS4-1). Finally in fourth grade, students combine what they learned in second and third grade, and they are expected to "identify evidence from patterns in rock formations and fossils in rock layers to support an explanation for changes in a landscape over time" (4-ESS1-1).

These standards are critical to students understanding a central aspect of evolutionary theory—the requisite time needed for evolution to account for the diversity of life on Earth. Much of the criticism of evolution instruction is based upon the belief in a young Earth. According to young-Earth creationists, Earth is between 6,000 and 12,000 years old. By contrast, evolutionary theory (informed by geology, paleontology, chemistry, oceanography, and other fields of science) asserts that life began on the planet approximately 4 billion years ago. Only with such a long period of time could evolutionary forces account for the diversity of life (both extant and extinct) on Earth.

HOW WHAT STUDENTS LEARN ABOUT SCIENCE RELATES TO THE EVOLUTION CONTENT

Note how the characteristics of science, described earlier in this chapter, relate to this foundational content about evolution. For example, concepts related to inheritance are included as early as first grade, when students are learning that traits they observe in organisms are not randomly derived but rather passed from parent to offspring. Even very young learners can make observations and then analyze, interpret, and use these observations as evidence to support this idea.

Similarly, with regards to adaptations and natural selection, we see the importance of evidence in explaining patterns of physical characteristics of organisms and the impact this has on organisms' survival. Prior to Charles Darwin identifying natural selection as the mechanism of evolution, his contemporary Jean-Baptiste Lamarck proposed the inheritance of acquired characteristics. Darwin was able to provide evidence to support his idea while Lamarck could not. This represents how scientists share their ideas with each other and how scientific ideas change with new evidence.

Finally, regarding the geologic time scale, we continue to see the importance of evidence. Students are tasked to use evidence to support the conclusion that Earth events can occur quickly or slowly. They are expected to analyze and interpret data to provide evidence about extinct organisms and their environment. Lastly, students are expected to identify evidence from patterns to support explanations for changes in landscapes over time.

Although not directly stated in the standards identified above, teachers are tasked with ensuring that students explicitly understand that science is limited to the natural world. The observations and patterns used as evidence in science were made in the natural world. As such, science is limited to natural phenomena and natural explanations of them. This characteristic of science is critically important for discerning science from non-science, particularly when it comes to interactions between scientific and religious claims.

> *"In the current age of alternative facts and the war on science, teachers are the first line of defense to ensure their students acquire scientific literacy. In our increasingly scientific society, such educational outcomes are critical."*

IMPLICATIONS AND CONCLUSIONS

You can see that we have discussed quite a bit about science and not nearly as much about religion in this chapter compared to some others in this book. There is a good reason for this. We believe that understanding the characteristics of science is vital for understanding scientific content such as evolution and for preparing students to discern scientific and religious points of view as they grow and mature. Teachers who have the tools to distinguish science from non-science can limit their science teaching to what legitimately belongs. Further, teachers will be armed with the language necessary to articulate this distinction in such a way that no judgment of merit is placed on faith-based beliefs. Rather, teachers can explain to students, parents, colleagues, and administrators why ideas such as creationism and intelligent design do not fit the requirements of being considered scientific and, therefore, have no place in a science curriculum.

Using the characteristics of science to evaluate the appropriateness of material to consider from a scientific perspective will serve students throughout their further educa-tion (think climate change and biotechnology) and their lives outside the classroom (think communicable disease prevention and genetic medicine). In the current age of alterna-tive facts and the war on science, teachers are the first line of defense to ensure that their students acquire scientific literacy. In our increasingly scientific society, such educational outcomes are critical.

REFERENCES

Banilower, E. R., P. S. Smith, K. A. Malzahn, C. L. Plumley, E. M. Gordon, and M. L. Hayes. 2018. *Report of the 2018 National Survey of Science and Mathematics Education+*. Chapel Hill, NC: Horizon Research. *http://horizon-research.com/NSSME*.

Binns, I. C., and M. A. Bloom. 2017. Distinguishing science from non-science: Preservice elementary teachers' perspectives on evolution, creationism, and intelligent design. *International Journal of Educational Methodology* 3 (1): 1–15. doi:10.12973/ijem.3.1.1.

Bloom, M. A., and I. C. Binns. 2018. Yes, elementary school teachers also need to know evolution. *Reports of the National Center for Science Education* 38 (2): 3–5.

Mallapaty, S. 2018. Paper authorship goes hyper. *Nature Index* (January 30). *www.natureindex.com*.

National Academy of Sciences and Institute of Medicine. 2008. *Science, evolution, and creationism*. Washington, DC: National Academies Press.

NGSS Lead States. 2013. *Next Generation Science Standards: For states, by states*. Washington, DC: National Academies Press. *www.nextgenscience.org/next-generation-science-standards*.

Science and Religion in Middle School and High School Classrooms

Lee Meadows, Lindsey Porter, Nathan Einsig, and Josh Hubbard

This chapter brings us to the heart of the conflict around teaching evolution—the classrooms of middle and high school teachers across America. These are the classrooms where science teachers have to bring all of the issues, in evolution and beyond, home to their actual teaching practices as they engage students in learning about and making sense of evolution and other topics with potentially religious implications.

Many American science teachers know the issues faced by students who are resistant to learning about evolution. We have seen them struggle. We have had a student raise her hand and say, "You mean God didn't create the world?" We have seen a little bit of fear in her eyes. We have watched a bright student take his first zero ever because he would not even attempt the evolution test. We may have been impressed with his zeal but saddened by the impact on his academic record. We have tried patiently to answer the same objections period after period from the students who had been given a list of "Questions to Ask Your Teacher About Evolution." We could tell that those students were wholeheartedly devoted to a life-or-death battle as they had been taught. We know now that, for many of our students, studying evolution goes beyond science and touches on issues much bigger than just fossils and change over time.

Some of us may also dread the evolution unit about as much as our students do. Those of us who teach middle school know how important it is to nurture our students through the life changes they are facing and how confusing their lives can be at times. Those of us who teach high school know how important it is to guide our students to solidify their understandings of science in the last biology course they will probably take. For middle and high school students, the topic of evolution can actually increase the confusion and conflict in their lives, and sometimes we may be tempted to wonder if teaching the topic is necessary or even appropriate.

The problems we face may not necessarily be due to evolution itself, however. They may be due to big-picture issues pressing on teachers and students from outside the classroom, as this book has been laying out. They can also be due to internal issues inside the classroom, especially with the approach that some science teachers take. This chapter brings together some of those external and internal issues into an overview of a different teaching approach, one that offers a method for engaging students without threatening their personal beliefs. We begin by introducing ourselves as authors, so you can know a little about the journeys that brought us to teaching evolution and the kinds of classrooms we teach in. We then provide eight practical strategies we have found to be effective for both teaching science with integrity and respecting the worldviews of each of our students.

OUR JOURNEYS TO A COMMON TEACHING APPROACH

As authors of this chapter, we came to a common teaching approach through different journeys. Lee grew up in fundamentalist Christianity in north Mississippi. He was the kid who asked about faith issues in biology class and about science issues in church youth group. He was also the kid who learned those questions were not welcome in either place! When Lee began to realize as an adult that he did not need to come to a nice, clean resolution of his faith and science, he began to get traction on the personal conflict he had felt about evolution. This traction propelled him to two decades of work with science teachers in the American South to help them understand that they can teach evolution well without throwing religious students into turmoil. Lee works as a science teacher educator at an Alabama university, he writes and speaks on the teaching of evolution, and his book *The Missing Link: An Inquiry Approach for Teaching All Students About Evolution* (Meadows 2009) lays out a pathway for teaching evolution in public school settings where students may have strong, personal objections.

Nathan remembers as a 13-year-old middle school kid waiting in line in at a restaurant after church witnessing an exchange between his dad and a member of their congregation. Nathan's father taught biology and environmental science for a rural/suburban school district in Pennsylvania. In making conversation while waiting for a table, the church member inquired about how Nathan's dad circumvented the teaching of evolution in the public school setting. His stark and matter-of-fact response ended the conversation as fast as it began: "I don't. I teach it because it is part of biology." Nathan remembers noticing the abrupt, bristling response from the church member and wondering what the big deal was. The topic of Earth history and evolution was one that Nathan eagerly studied as a child with the aid of his father. From a very young age Nathan was regularly going on fossil-hunting trips and scouring educational books and magazines for information on early humans, extinct species, and long-ago ages of Earth. This was all done with encouragement and loving support from his family. Never once did this information bump up against his church's teachings. For most of his childhood, Nathan saw the topics of Earth's natural history and religion as running parallel, never intersecting until that afternoon while waiting for a table to open at the local diner. From then on, he started to notice and engage in conversations about the confluence of science and religion. What he did not realize at the time was that his dad defused a potentially tense conversation by being up front about the nature of science, an approach Nathan has used through his teaching career in the geosciences and as a high school department chairperson in Mechanicsburg, Pennsylvania, where he and Lindsey work together.

Like several other authors, Lindsey grew up within a fundamentalist tradition and, although she excelled in school, stubbornly clung to a belief that scientists were, at best, wrong and, at worst, in cahoots with the devil to deceive students about the origins of the world and life in it. In choosing a Christian liberal arts college to pursue a biology degree, however, Lindsey was finally exposed to an environment that fostered an exploration of science and religion without setting them up as opposed to each other. She attended church with deacons who doubled as her professors of evolutionary biology, and for her capstone course, she analyzed the history of conflict, as well as nonconflict, between science and religion. As a young teacher, Lindsey was worried about encountering students who would voice their disagreement and protest her lessons as she had done. However, such public defiance never occurred. Instead, Lindsey would only discover her students' discomfort with issues of science and religion when they let slip their beliefs in quiet protest by writing religious explanations for natural phenomena intended to be explained scientifically. Lindsey was often surprised by these instances, but each has helped inform her ever-evolving approach to teaching controversial topics in science class.

Josh's teaching journey is different from the other authors because he teaches in a conservative Christian school in Michigan. His key shift has been his move to an inquiry-centered teaching environment. Josh started as a very traditional teacher, designing his teaching so that he would lecture to his students on what scientific research says about evolution in order to build a strong case. He began to realize, however, that he was designing instruction for himself, not for his students. Josh admits that at the beginning he was not very good at teaching by inquiry, struggling to create solid inquiry experiences for his students. Lee's book was really helpful to Josh, giving him a framework to apply it to his situation and challenging him to turn over the classroom to his students. He and his students began to research questions together, discuss the evidence they discovered, and make claims based on their supporting evidence. Furthermore, Josh's context of an entire population of students resistant to learning about evolution offers wisdom to public school teachers in similar situations. When he teaches evolution, Josh faces the challenge of how to direct a classroom full of students, who are almost all diametrically opposed to the concept, to begin to consider the evidence for it. He consistently works to respect the genuine issues his students have with evolution while still guiding them to ask questions, investigate, argue from evidence, and reflect on their understanding—a process he has found requires a deep commitment to designing backwards (McTighe and Wiggins 2013) from the goal that his students understand, not believe in, evolution.

Lee and Josh met over a decade ago at a National Science Teaching Association conference and have been in conversation about teaching evolution ever since.

OUR APPROACH: UNDERSTANDING EVOLUTION WITHOUT HAVING TO BELIEVE IT

Consider a teaching approach that guides students to understand evolution but not necessarily to believe it. This is the overall approach we want you to consider because it is at the heart of engaging students who resist learning about evolution without threatening their worldview. This approach might be a new idea because you have thought that resolving students' conflicts was the only option.

You probably know the resolution approach, even if you have never heard that term. It demands that beliefs about supernatural and scientific understandings have to be resolved. If scientific evidence conflicts with what religion teaches, then one of them is wrong, and teachers have to show students which one is in error. Unless you jumped straight into this chapter when you picked up this book, you know now that focusing on resolution is not a good idea. In our approach, teachers open up the classroom by allowing students to examine the scientific evidence for evolution, and how scientists explain that evidence, through intentionally designing learning activities to diffuse the pressure that students feel to resolve the conflict. Some highly resistant students might not accept any of the evidence or explanations they encounter, and some may accept portions only. The evolution unit can still be successful, though, because its instructional goal should be for all students to understand, not believe in, evolution.

In this approach, students consistently hear their teachers say, "I expect you to understand evolution, but I do not expect you necessarily to believe it." Teachers affirm the value and beauty of students' personal beliefs while also guiding them to examine the evidence for evolution and its place as a powerful scientific explanation. Teachers support students in the hard intellectual work of encountering the support for and implications of evolutionary theory, but the teachers also recognize that for many students, this can be threatening. At the bottom line, teachers do not seek to overturn students' religious beliefs.

This approach requires us to honor our students' beliefs. Religion is not something to be stamped out of the science classroom, but that agenda is what the resolution approach often communicates. If children hear us say, "We're not going to talk about faith; we're going to stick to the science," they may hear us saying, "Your faith is not important." That may be the furthest thing from our minds, but because secondary school students are sensitive to rejection, they typically sense their faith being denigrated if we refuse to acknowledge how their understandings about evolution and their religious beliefs can be intertwined.

TEACHING STRATEGIES FOR UNDERSTANDING, NOT BELIEVING

Our overall approach of teaching evolution for understanding, not believing, gives the big picture of what teaching evolution to resistant students looks like. Next, we provide you with several practical strategies that we have worked out in our own teaching. Nathan and Lindsey developed many of these strategies to lower the threat level in their biology and Earth science classrooms and to foster a tentative willingness on the part of such students to question and learn. Josh developed other strategies as he was implementing the general ideas from Lee's book. Taken as a whole, these strategies seek to avoid triggering students' fears of being asked to choose between their faith and learning science, while planting the seeds of scientific thinking in hopes that acceptance of science will bloom alongside students' intellectual maturity, bearing fruit in their adult lives that they may not be ready for in high school. At the end of this chapter, we include a list of resources you can tap to help implement these strategies in your classroom.

Strategy 1: Emphasize Stories From the History of Science

As the amount of scientific knowledge has expanded over the years, the challenge to cover all the science standards has intensified and lessons surrounding the history of science have tended to diminish. Lindsey and Nathan find great value, however, in sharing the stories of scientific discoveries (see Chapter 2 for additional information), particularly those fostering empathy for people whose discoveries seemed to contradict their prior notions of the world. These stories humanize the process of science and model for students the ways scientists operate without yet having it all figured out. These anecdotes do not have to take too much time away from other content. They can serve as bell-ringer reading assignments, short discussion points during direct instruction, student jigsaw activities, or even as background material for assessment prompts.

A classic example from biology is Charles Darwin's hesitance to publish his work on natural selection, which can be structured into a classroom discussion of his motives for both the delay and his ultimate decision to publish. In Earth science, it is helpful to teach students about the steady-state notion of the universe and the famous thinkers who subscribed to it, including Robert Wilson, discoverer of cosmic background radiation, and Albert Einstein with his cosmological constant. An anecdote does not need to rely on such a dramatic challenge to worldview, however, to be helpful. Biology students can empathize with Gregor Mendel when given the opportunity to contemplate what would motivate a monk to count so many peas and whether his discoveries might have challenged his ideas about the role of God in nature. Earth science students can empathize with early efforts to calculate the age of the Earth. Students can use these historical examples to illustrate the scientific approach to problem solving and identify where bias, assumptions, or lack of information limited the accuracy of their results, as was the case for Lord Kelvin's estimation of the age of the Earth calculated before the discovery of radioactivity. And middle school teachers can carefully select stories to connect with their students' unique developmental needs.

Strategy 2: Tap Into the Power of Effective Questioning

Josh and Lee both consistently tap into the power of questions to help engage their students. Josh begins the evolution unit with a question that Lee developed: "Why can't we just skip evolution?" He finds this a powerful question because of his students' viewpoint of evolution as a completely invalid perspective on the world. They easily disengage from this core piece of the scientific worldview, especially when taught with traditional pedagogy. This question places the focus back on Josh's students, allowing them to develop the ideas necessary to answer the question.

After Josh poses the question, he gives students time to develop their first thoughts individually and then to share those with partners, groups, and the class. This allows him to get a sense of student thinking as the unit begins. This process also starts creating the key classroom environmental piece of students both responding to questions and asking their own. He takes time to lead students in listing things they already think they know about evolution and to develop questions they need to answer if the class is going to understand, but not believe in, evolution. He usually gets very specific questions about different parts of evolution such as timelines, dinosaurs, and apes.

Next, Josh finds it helpful to organize the questions and to direct the class to the first major question they are going to investigate. Most students know some things about evolution, which allows him to introduce another question that Lee developed: "What does evolution actually say?" Students then write their responses in their journals. This is very important because at the end of the unit he will ask them the same question again. Students then see the changes in their own thinking, a powerful metacognitive activity that we highly recommend.

Strategy 3: Value Questions Over Answers

Nathan and Lindsey extend the emphasis on questioning to placing value on questions that students raise on their own. Too frequently the science curriculum is pruned to only discoveries leading to the successful theories of today, but Nathan and Lindsey find great value in sharing the dead ends of scientific thinking that have occurred along the way. Science is not a linear path of right answers, but a web of discoveries and insights that have survived despite the limitations and biases of the people doing the science.

Students feeling their religious beliefs threatened can find some tension eased when their teachers shift the focus away from having answers and toward having questions. Science and religion are often presented as different ways of knowing, but students can still struggle if the things they know based on their religion seem to be at odds with the things they know based on what they learn in science class. They can sense that they will eventually be forced to choose which "truth" is right. When teachers speak of science as a way of knowing, they may miss an opportunity to present science as a process of questioning, testing, and discovering. Teachers should emphasize that, while science classes require students to gain the background in what is currently known in science, this is a mere jumping-off point for the real work of science, namely asking the next question and devising a way to go about finding out even more.

Teachers who hope to nurture an environment open to questioning must themselves be willing and unafraid to be questioned and must resist the temptation to pretend to have all of the answers. Middle school teachers are well aware of the challenging and even heart-wrenching questions their students can raise as they face the challenges of early adolescence and of the comfort that teachers can bring as they guide their students in courageously facing tough questions. In Mechanicsburg, Pennsylvania, Lindsey and Nathan encounter a significant number of students attending public school for the first time in ninth grade. These students have grown accustomed to having their curiosity answered with "because God …" in their parochial education. These students find it discomforting, but also enticing, to instead have their questions praised and even met with still other questions they have not yet considered.

Strategy 4: Directly Contrast the Vocabulary of Science With Everyday Language

Students learning about evolution are often confused by the language scientists use to describe their process of thinking. Almost all students come to science class with common-language understandings of words such as *theory*, *law*, and *fact* not matching the way these words are used in the more formal context of science. Unfortunately, scientists are also ordinary people who use these terms in a common-language fashion from time to time, and the lack of consistency can perpetuate confusion. *Theory* is certainly the most misunderstood of these terms, signifying to most students merely an idea or a hunch. To suggest that evolution, Big Bang, or molecular genetics are merely theories in that sense is one of the most common defense mechanisms against science. These words must be clarified early in a course and repeatedly reinforced throughout the year (see the nature of science discussion in Chapter 1).

In ninth-grade Earth science classes, Lindsey and Nathan have students first complete a self-assessment of their understanding of these terms. Students are given their scores but not told which questions they answered incorrectly. Confronting their misconceptions at the start helps prevent student overconfidence and their tuning out the lesson. Students then complete a jigsaw activity in which they learn about both the common and scientific uses of five tricky words: *hypothesis*, *theory*, *law*, *belief*, and *fact*. Students complete an organizer comparing and contrasting the two styles of usage of one of these terms and prepare to teach a group of their peers how to correctly use their term in the scientific context. After the jigsaw, groups work together to find examples online of individuals misusing one of the words as well as an example of the word being used in the scientific sense. Students discuss how everyday citizens could be confused about the significance of a scientific idea and then brainstorm ways that scientists, the media, and even teachers could help make communication clearer. Because the word *theory* seems to cause the most trouble in high school science classes, the lesson concludes with an overview of some of the less controversial, and more familiar, theories in science—such as germ theory of disease, cell theory, plate tectonic theory, atomic theory, and general relativity—before considering evolutionary theory or Big Bang theory.

While such a lesson early in the year goes a long way to clarifying the confidence scientists have in various ideas, Nathan and Lindsey have found misconceptions to be stubborn things. They must reinforce the meaning and correct usage of these words frequently during any science class in order for students to transfer the information to future experiences. They have to take time whenever they present a new hypothesis, theory, or law to reassess and, if necessary, reteach the scientific uses of such terms. If someone in a video clip or reading passage uses one of these terms, students do a quick evaluation on whether the word was used in the common-language or scientific sense. Nathan and Lindsey emphasize in each case that nothing is wrong with using these words casually, but that in science class they will ask students to strive to do so scientifically at all times to be clear.

Strategy 5: Respect Students' Journeys in Assignments and Tests

Just as students are asked to use words precisely in the scientific context during class, teachers must also select language that is clear and respectful of the potential struggle students might be having with the material. Words have power and students who may seem to be faring well with what for them is a controversial bit of science may hit their limit when asked to write their thoughts down or to speak in public about a subject. When asked how the Moon formed, for example, students feeling a conflict between their religious ideas and the science they have been learning may see this as a test of faith. Teachers who ask questions in this way are probably not trying to prompt a choice between students' faith and their grades, but they may be unaware they have put the student in a bind until they see for themselves a disconcerting answer explaining what the Bible or other religious texts have taught them.

"Ultimately, when students are allowed to walk between both worlds, they stand a much greater chance of understanding and accepting scientific ways of thinking."

Lindsey and Nathan have created and revised assignments and assessments that specifically avoid triggering the need for students to sacrifice their grade in order to remain faithful and that still assess students' understanding of the content. A typical assessment on the Big Bang might ask students, "How did the universe begin and change over time? Include three lines of evidence that support your answer." Instead, it is better to ask, "Scientists draw on three lines of evidence to explain the formation and early evolution of the universe. Name and describe each, including its role in developing Big Bang theory." The shift in these questions is subtle and many students would not notice it. The first version asks students to state how the universe began for which they might have two answers, one known from religion and the other from science class. The second version specifically asks about the evidence that scientists use and avoids forcing the student to choose a religious belief in that moment. A student who fervently believes the universe began in a supernatural way can still truthfully answer the question and demonstrate his or her learning.

Even with carefully constructed questions, Lindsey and Nathan have had occasions when a student answered in a religious sense. They use these as opportunities to have a conversation with the student to clarify how they do not intend to force students to choose between their beliefs and learning science. They point out the intentional wording of assignment and test questions to the student as an example of their commitment to honoring students' journeys as learners and a sign of respect that they deserve the space and freedom to learn new science without being required to discard or compromise articles of their faith. Similar conversations have helped concerned parents feel more at ease with this approach to science instruction, even when it seems to conflict with their views. Ultimately, when students are allowed to walk between both worlds, they stand a much greater chance of understanding and accepting scientific ways of thinking.

Strategy 6: Engage Students With Actual Evidence for Species Evolution

Josh has developed a series of lessons on whale evolution, which he calls the poster child for evolution, because he has seen the power of engaging his students with actual evidence. Josh's goals with this strategy are to direct his students to locate scientific evidence, to describe it in both graphical and textual ways, and, finally, to be able to answer from a scientific worldview, "What does evolution actually say about whales?" His students typically respond well to this strategy. They often exit the unit not accepting evolution, but they do come to understand evolution because of the way the lessons are designed with an inquiry approach placing a priority on students' learning and presenting actual scientific evidence.

Josh begins the lessons with a video clip, "Great Transformations," from the Public Broadcasting System's (PBS; 2018) *Evolution* series. As his students watch the first 16 minutes, he asks them to write down the pieces of evidence Dr. Phil Gingerich used to develop his theory of whale evolution. Josh then leads a classroom discussion on what students think so far, which is a good opportunity to check in and invite student questions about the claims that were made. After Josh has established a baseline understanding about whale evolution, he has students gather evidence on the variety of different whales mentioned in the video through a timeline activity. Most of his students have not heard of these different types of whales. He gives each student group one copy of the Whale Evolution Data Table Worksheet, a blank graphic organizer found on the same PBS website, and they work together to collect information and to complete the table.

Josh then does two additional activities to help them see both the order of whale evolution and the reason for that order. The first one is a simple presentation in which each group must claim a slide in a Google Slides presentation and present on a specific organism in the whale lineage. This creates an opportunity for the students to own the evidence and reasoning as well as gives Josh a formative assessment opportunity on their research. Students are assessed on how they show the evidence for where in the whale lineage their assigned organism should be placed, what features this organism has that are different or new, and why the organism should be considered a link in whale evolution. Josh's students are now ready for a fuller layout of the whale evolution story line. Next, he has them watch a section of "Fossils, Genes, and Mousetraps," a lecture by Dr. Ken Miller (Howard Hughes Medical Institute 2018) on whale evolution, so they see and hear the evidence they have been deciphering on their own. Josh then guides his students to develop a complete whale evolution timeline, and he has done this several different ways: He has given them paper and pencils to draw it, they have used computers to research pictures that they printed out and glued onto paper, and they have used web-based timeline generators.

At this point, Josh's students have a solid informational base on what scientific evidence says for whale evolution. He ends the lesson series by guiding his students to revisit their original journal entries with the question, "What do you think now?" He enjoys seeing their growth in making statements supported by scientific evidence and he really likes to hear his students making statements along the lines of "I used to think this … but now I think this." Josh encourages them to write down new questions or things they are wondering about. He may not have class time to investigate all of their questions, but some can be answered with additional readings or video clips.

Strategy 7: Weave Controversial Topics Throughout the Entire Course

A single exposure to any concept is rarely enough for students to gain mastery or total understanding. The same is true for potentially upsetting concepts such as evolution and origins, whether it be the origins of life, the Earth, or the entire universe. In too many biology and life science classrooms, evolution is taught as a stand-alone unit with few connections to the rest of the curriculum. Teaching in this way gives the wrong impression of evolution's place within biology and suggests it could be removed from the course entirely without affecting the rest, like some sort of tumor. When evolution is taught in this way, students are more likely to dread the start of the unit or even prepare themselves to resist accepting anything during those lessons. Students' defenses are up; they are prepared for battle. For some, the battle may be silently enduring the lessons, while others may feel compelled to publicly challenge the teacher, boycott activities or tests, or otherwise cause disruption.

Besides causing these students undue stress and unhappiness, this approach to teaching biology neglects the elegance of evolutionary theory's role throughout the entire field of biology. There should certainly be a unit in the biology course in which evolution is explained, including its discovery, mechanisms, and predictions. This must not, however, be the students' first exposure to these ideas. Instead, Lindsey and Nathan have found the power in seizing every opportunity to mention evolution's role. In a unit on cell structure, for example, the endosymbiotic theory for the origin of organelles such as chloroplasts and mitochondria provides a small dose of how evolution works. Later, teachers can revisit these ideas in a unit on cellular energetics and guide students to compare the functions of mitochondria and chloroplasts in cellular respiration and photosynthesis to the strategies that unicellular organisms use to make or acquire their energy. During a unit on DNA, teachers can continue to develop these ideas as students learn how the genetic material of their mitochondria is fundamentally different than that of their cell nuclei, yet in many ways similar to that of bacteria. Units on cellular reproduction and genetics provide students the mechanisms for genetic diversity and the introduction of novel traits via mutations.

The approach for middle school teachers is similar even though middle school standards focus more on natural selection than on evolution of species. During a unit on ecosystems, teachers can point to natural selection as a powerful way to understand interdependent relationships and a pattern of interactions. In a unit on growth and reproduction of organisms, middle school teachers can help their students see how natural selection is an elegant way to develop arguments and scientific reasoning for reproduction and genetics.

With this strategy, students will have already begun to build a foundation of understanding of evolution that stands a better chance of developing further during an evolution unit than if the theory had been avoided and then taught in isolation. Teaching biology in this way reinforces how evolution is not merely a topic within biology, but one of its principle components—a thread that cannot be removed without unraveling the whole.

Strategy 8: Create Department Policy Regarding the Teaching of Controversial Topics

As Nathan began his teaching career at Mechanicsburg Area Senior High School in Mechanicsburg, he found himself just a few miles away from Dover, Pennsylvania, a district and community embroiled in the landmark *Kitzmiller et al. v. Dover Area School District* (2005) trial dealing with the issue of intelligent design in the science classroom (see Chapters 2, 3, and 5 for more detail). He quickly found the local community and district educators to be abuzz about the trial. He worked with his mentor and department chair at the time, Michael Floreck, to draft a position statement on intelligent design that could be used by department teachers and school administrators if parents and students inquired about the topic. A few years later, Nathan became the science department chair and used an updated position statement on reasons not to include intelligent design or other nonscientific explanations in Mechanicsburg's curriculum. He used this position statement to educate families, administrators, and colleagues on the differences between valid, empirically based science research and faith-based explanations.

Science teachers and administrators need to be on the same page with respect to what is and is not appropriate for the science classroom. Position statements like the one used in Mechanicsburg are an excellent tool for establishing a baseline in communicating with parents and the public. We provide the statement here (see Figure 7.1) so that you can review it as you begin to consider what a similar policy might look like in your school district.

Figure 7.1. Mechanicsburg Area Senior High School science department position statement

Science is the search for natural explanations to the phenomena we encounter in our daily lives; it is accomplished by applying the scientific method to such problems. When science is implemented correctly, a researcher never allows his or her own biases to influence their results. A continuum of certainty exists within science and the word "theory" holds a very specific meaning. While a person may use the word "theory" in common speech to mean a hunch, or a guess, this is much closer to our definition of a hypothesis. Scientific problem solving begins by offering an educated guess, the so-called hypothesis, and attempting to test it against a control. If the hypothesis, in addition to many other similar hypotheses, becomes validated, the idea begins to build toward the status of a scientific theory. These theories are the pinnacle of scientific understanding with regard to how a system or phenomenon in nature works. Darwin's initial theory was published over 150 years ago. Since then, evolution has withstood repeated scrutiny by both the scientific community and the public. While our modern understanding of genetics and cell biology show the mechanics of evolution in a way that Darwin did not know, the observation and accuracy of the theory of evolution hold true and are bolstered by these discoveries. Evolutionary theory has accomplished this increasing level of certainty for the past century and is a widely accepted fundamental theory of biological science.

While many people disagree with the implications of evolutionary theory, it is still a sound theory, and one that is a central theme in biological science. Intelligent design (ID) does not meet the qualifications necessary to be considered a scientific theory; it is in fact, much more like a hypothesis. While it does offer some very difficult challenges to Darwinian natural selection, scientists have responded by continuing to find answers to those questions. In turn, ID does not produce a testable hypothesis, but merely asserts that a designer must have been present to aid the process. The Mechanicsburg science staff feels very strongly that Darwinian natural selection is the only valid scientific explanation for the trends seen in the fossil record and in the genetic code of Earth's diverse forms of life. The theory has not been damaged by arguments (such as irreducible complexity) proposed by ID advocates in such a way as to become prohibitive. Until ID begins to produce a verifiable hypothesis, it is not a scientific theory, and will not be addressed as such in our science classrooms. Since the topic is likely to come up, we are willing to discuss its shortcomings as a scientific theory, and the obvious agenda of its proponents, but will not offer it as a viable alternative to Darwin's theory.

It must also be said that we do not believe that evolutionary theory and religion are mutually exclusive; in other words, belief in one does not prohibit belief in the other. We feel that it is necessary to teach our students the current scientific consensus and allow them to decide for themselves based upon the scientific evidence presented. Since we have limited time available to discuss this topic and those issues related to it, we will not plan on discussing every point of contention made by the ID proponents. However, if students or their parents are interested in having a point-by-point discussion on the merits of evolutionary theory and modern research as well as the accusations that are part of ID thought, questions can be directed toward the teacher and/or department coordinator and time can be made after school hours to discuss these issues. Students will need to rely upon influences outside of science class to foster an understanding of those ideas not considered within the domain of science.

We recommend that your science department, at a minimum, consider building a statement like this for any topics you find potentially controversial. Mechanicsburg is currently developing a broader document to include climate science, deep time, origins of life, and origins of the universe, as well as evolution. The discussions within the department alone are worth the effort. Being able to vet ideas, construct common language, share stories, and commiserate builds unity and understanding with colleagues and is in itself a most valuable endeavor.

CONCLUSION

Teaching evolution does not have to create a war in the classroom. Science teachers truly can do both: teach science well, evolution in particular, and respect the religious beliefs of their students, even those whose faith creates conflict for them. Our overall approach gives science teachers a way to move beyond conflict and toward a classroom honoring both science and students' cultural and religious backgrounds. The strategies we have developed offer practical applications in line with our overall approach and examples you can follow in developing your own strategies for engaging resistant students in learning evolution and other scientific concepts.

In recent years, we are seeing some changes in the landscape of evolution education in American schools. Nathan and Lindsey have noticed a shift in the climate of their classrooms. Students no longer seem to arrive in August primed for a fight, and it has been years since either of them has seen a student write a religious explanation for a scientific phenomenon on an assignment or test. At the same time, both have experienced an increase in the number of students mentioning their religion in a nonconfrontational way. More students come in and talk about their background and ask questions out of curiosity and with trust that they will receive honest and compassionate answers and conversation in return. Lee is seeing at a national level a real decrease in the number of teachers who advocate a check-your-religion-at-the-door approach to teaching evolution, and maybe even a rising tide of science teachers and science educators who want to see confrontation removed from evolution education.

The strategies above will certainly need to evolve as the population and culture of teenagers shift, but the core approach of teaching controversial science topics for understanding, not belief, will remain effective. An emphasis on decreasing conflict while increasing thinking, understanding, and empathy will make the teaching of evolution, deep time, and even climate change something that all students and teachers can approach without fear.

REFERENCES

Howard Hughes Medical Institute. 2018. Fossils, genes, and mousetraps. *www.hhmi.org/biointeractive/fossils-genes-and-mousetraps*.

Kitzmiller et al. v. Dover Area School District, 400 F. Supp. 2d 707 (M.D. Pa. 2005).

McTighe, J., and G. Wiggins 2013. *Essential questions: Opening doors to student understanding.* Alexandria, VA: ASCD.

Meadows, L. 2009. *The missing link: An inquiry approach for teaching all students about evolution.* Portsmouth, NH: Heinemann.

Public Broadcasting System (PBS). 2018. Evolution lab. *www.pbs.org/wgbh/nova/labs/lab/evolution*.

RESOURCES

"Big History Project," *https://school.bighistoryproject.com*

"Classroom Resources," *www.hhmi.org/biointeractive/evolution-collection*

"Evolution Resources," *www.nas.edu/evolution*

"Teaching Evolution Through Human Examples," *http://humanorigins.si.edu/education/teaching-evolution-through-human-examples*

Science and Religion in Higher Education

Lisa Borgerding

I don't believe in evolution. ... I'm Christian.
—College science learner

Religion challenges nearly every aspect of geology and is a completely separate entity that does not need to be included with scientific teaching.
—College science instructor

I think it's kind of best to teach evolution and let the students understand that you're not necessarily saying that religion's not a real thing or anything, but you kind of [have to] separate that science aspect from that religion aspect.
—Preservice science teacher

The elephant in the room for this college science learner, college science faculty member, and preservice science teacher, based on my interviews with them, is clearly religion. Specifically, questions about the relationship between science and religion are particularly important for college science learners and preservice science teachers who confront science content that appears contradictory to doctrinal religious teachings. In this chapter, I explore how religion surfaces in science teaching and learning in higher education contexts. First, I explore models of college student development in terms of epistemology, noting how college students often begin seeking authority and eventually graduate with more relativistic views of knowledge. Second, I describe research findings and stories from college science faculty related to challenges and promising approaches for navigating religion in college science classes. Third, I investigate the specific case of preservice science teacher education in higher education. Finally, I conclude with some recommendations for higher education faculty for mitigating science-religion tensions.

Before diving into these issues of science and religion in higher education, I should provide some of my own context for readers to understand my perspective. I was raised in a loosely Catholic home, and science and religion were never in conflict for me personally. Through my undergraduate biology major coursework, religion was invisible; and evolution, Big Bang theory, and radiometric dating were never questioned. My first real awareness of science-religion conflicts occurred during my student teaching when my cooperating teacher suggested I avoid teaching the evolution chapter, even maintaining that the chapter on reproduction would be less socially controversial for some religious students in the district!

When I was hired as a high school biology teacher in 2000, I was the first teacher at my rural high school to teach evolution. My students did indeed face religious conflicts. During my first year of teaching, before I had ever even mentioned the *E* word, a well-intentioned student informed me, "Miss B, Darwin is the devil." I came to realize I played a delicate and important role in these students' lives as another student pleaded with me, "Miss B, just tell us what you think so we'll know what to think." My evolution instruction expanded to include the nature of science (NOS) and small-group discussions of science-religion distinctions.

These experiences fueled my doctoral work and still motivate me today as I prepare future secondary science teachers, provide science teacher professional development, and conduct research about the teaching and learning of evolution.

COLLEGE STUDENT EPISTEMOLOGICAL DEVELOPMENT

College students are on a journey about knowledge itself, often entering college with dualistic views of the world in which entities are either good or bad, knowledge is certain, and authorities are the source of knowledge. Along this journey, knowledge becomes less certain and more situation-dependent. How they understand knowledge is their epistemology, and several models of college student epistemological development exist. Some models assume that this development flows along a single trajectory, while other models treat it as multidimensional with development flowing along multiple trajectories (for a review, see Hofer and Pintrich 1997). William Perry (1970) advocated for a unidimensional model during which college students move along a trajectory in which knowledge becomes less certain, authorities are questioned, and notions of good and bad become highly contextualized. Perry loosely characterized these progressive phases as dualistic (there are right/wrong answers, and authorities should be obeyed); multiplistic (authorities have not resolved all the problems yet); relativistic (answers are uncertain and contextually dependent); and, finally, committed/dialectical (decision making is based on one's commitments in an uncertain world) stages of development.

What could all this mean for college science learners and college preservice science teachers? Given the vast body of scientific knowledge, we tend to set up our classes according to transmission models of learning (rather than constructivist). And the college students we teach may view us as authorities and gatekeepers of their future careers (e.g., "give me the answer" is a common refrain many of us hear), just like my high school student who wanted me to tell him what to think about evolution. College science learners' epistemological views also shade how they interpret scientific knowledge. In a previous study (Borgerding, Deniz, and Anderson 2017), my colleagues and I found that Perry dualists and multiplists more often appealed to authorities for their evolution positions, were less accepting of evolution, and less often viewed evolution as an example of good science. We interpret this to mean that biology learners view evolution differently based on their epistemological ideas about the source of knowledge (authorities such as the Bible, a college professor, or a parent), justification (what counts as good science), and the certainty (or tentativeness) of science.

Students' religious views interact with their broad epistemological tendencies with important implications for science learning. Some of the science content we teach contradicts students' religious teachings, and this represents a clash of two important authorities for dualists: their religious leaders and their college instructors. As students become further engaged in the practices of science (gathering evidence, making tentative claims, considering multiple explanations, making conclusions without 100% certainty), their assumption of the certainty of knowledge is tested. In a course that emphasized NOS and relationships between science and religion, some learners deferred to science, maintaining that the role of God was diminished if one accepted evidence contrary to nonliteral Genesis accounts, while others deferred more to religion upon learning that the claims of science were limited and not necessarily in conflict with religious authority (Martin-Hansen 2008). Clearly, as college students are pushed to address questions of authority, certainty of knowledge, and context, their personal religious views influence how they view science. We college educators must appreciate our role in these students' epistemological journeys as we help them explore new ideas and compare the merits of opposing ideas.

COLLEGE STUDENT RELIGIOUS BELIEFS AND SCIENCE CLASSES

College science learners bring their religious worldviews and understandings to their science classes and hold a range of positions regarding the relationships between science and religion. Students may hold science and religion to be entirely incompatible, compatible because of non-overlap, compatible because of integration, or several intermediary positions (Loving and Foster 2000; Shipman et al. 2002). In two separate studies of undergraduate biology students, about 25% of the students believed that one cannot accept evolution and believe in God (Findley, Lindsey, and Watts 2001), a view that does not change with science instruction alone (Sinclair, Pendarvis, and Baldwin 1997). Holding this incompatibility view, many religious students retain their identities by rejecting the science they perceive as conflicting with their doctrinal views. The college science learner quoted at the beginning of this chapter is exactly this kind of student, and she went on to tell me she just listened to the lectures without believing a word in her upper-level evolution class.

Students' religious beliefs and interpretations of their own religious doctrines have important consequences, sometimes negative, for science learning. Religiosity was shown to be critically important in the Deep South as religious students showed less evolution understanding and made the least gains in understanding when compared to their nonreligious peers. These highly religious students in the Deep South reject evolution even while realizing that it is accepted within the scientific community (Rissler, Duncan, and Caruso 2014), clearly deferring to the authority of their religious doctrines. Yet, some students who appeal to their religious authorities are surprised to learn that their own religious authorities have taken a compatibility stance with respect to scientific understandings. For example, when Mormon college students better understood their faith's neutral position on evolution, they were more accepting of evolution (Manwaring et al. 2015).

Some religious students enter college with worldviews aligned with their religious or family authorities but change their ideas during their college coursework. For these religious students, the process of becoming more accepting of evolution is a source of two kinds of anxiety: an uncomfortable awareness that their prior beliefs are changing and apprehension about how they can defend their evolution acceptance to their parents (Winslow, Staver, and Scharmann 2011). Thus, accepting science can have both existential and social costs for conflicted students, and we college faculty must acknowledge that our students face real consequences for such shifts. These students described their growing acceptance of evolution to have been facilitated by several factors: accepting evolutionary evidence, developing nonliteral interpretations of biblical accounts (e.g., Book of Genesis), coming into a realization that evolutionary acceptance and salvation are not linked, and having a Christian professor role model who accepted evolution (Winslow, Staver, and Scharmann 2011).

College students often crave some acknowledgment of their religious views and the religious tensions they face when learning science. After course readings and discussions about science-religion relationships, science education graduate students concluded that discussions of religion are sometimes warranted in science classes. They asserted that NOS must be taught in science classes and students should realize that science alone is limited and useful in only certain contexts (Loving and Foster 2000; also refer to Chapter 1). I provide some suggestions for this approach in the final section.

How do college students' religious positions compare to their science professors' world-views? College faculty members, in general, may be similar to their students with respect to the importance of religion in their lives and daily prayer practice (Paz-y-Mino and Espinosa 2010). However, college science faculty may be less religious. Among Texas, Arizona, elite U.S. research institutions, and elite British college science professors (respectively), 57.4%, 63%, 71.2%, and 78% of them indicated that they did not believe in or were agnostic about God (Barnes and Brownell 2016; Ecklund and Scheitle 2007; Smith and Eve 2009; Stirrat and Cornwell 2013). Although some studies have identified differences in religious beliefs across disciplines (Stirrat and Cornwell 2013), others have noted that demographic features such as age, marital status, and presence of children explain more variance among scientists' religiosity (Ecklund and Scheitle 2007).

Despite the science-religion conflicts noted by students, college science faculty often do not see it as their job to teach about NOS and science-religion distinctions. In a study of Arizona college biology instructors, the vast majority said they do not address science-religion conflicts in their classes. For those who did address the conflict, most briefly mentioned religion to explain that religious ideas are not testable (Barnes and Brownell 2016). In a survey of natural scientists at a Midwestern university (Borgerding, unpublished data), I asked natural science faculty members about the extent to which they address distinctions between science and religion in their classes. Although 48.3% of the faculty indicated that science-religion relationships came up in their college science teaching, only 20.7% said they taught about science-religion relationships. Faculty offered many reasons for omitting these relationships. These reasons primarily centered on their desire to focus exclusively on science, but they also included the need to keep students' religious views private, their lack of expertise in theology, the assumption that students are addressing these distinctions elsewhere, and the position that religion is a challenge to science and should not be broached in science coursework. The second quote from the opening of this chapter illustrates this final reason. For the relatively few natural science faculty who did teach about science-religion distinctions, some described teaching about science and religion as two valuable worldviews, commenting on how evolution is not necessarily incompatible with religion, about the reliance of religion on faith and science on evidence, and about the need to articulate scientific evidence to a variety of audiences.

Innovative college science courses that do address science-religion distinctions have had positive effects. Courses on NOS, especially those that emphasize the bounded NOS, hold promise. Faculty in such classes make clear that science is limited to empirical questions and cannot be used to support or refute supernatural explanations. After instruction emphasizing how acceptance of a scientific theory does not necessarily preclude the existence of a supernatural entity, college freshmen were less anxious about learning about evolution. Some students with spiritual views integrated their religious understandings into scientific ones and others claimed that their faith was strengthened upon learning that evolution does not necessarily conflict with religion (Martin-Hansen 2008). These interventions need not be lengthy. In a college astronomy course that addressed science-religion distinctions for only a half-class session based on a reading that asserted that people can believe in both evolution and God, 59% of the students said they understood more about relationships between science, religion, and philosophy at the end of the course (Brickhouse et al. 2000). Similarly, in a Mormon university, a single class discussion about the church's neutral position on evolution had a significant impact on Mormon college students' evolution acceptance (Manwaring et al. 2015).

COLLEGE STUDENTS AND SCIENCE TEACHER EDUCATION

Many preservice science teachers face the same challenges as other college science learners, or perhaps more so, as education faculty and students tend to be more religious than their noneducation higher education peers (Long 2012). Surveys reveal that some preservice science teachers reject some or all aspects of evolution (Berkman and Plutzer 2011). Religiosity not only is important for the teaching of evolution, it affects the learning of other topics as well. Torres (2009) found that preservice teacher religiosity influenced beliefs about astronomy such as deferring to the biblical authority while maintaining that the Earth was the center of the universe, the sky is a dome, and the universe is 6,000 years old.

Teachers handle their science-religion conflicts in a number of ways: being unaware of, avoiding, being disturbed by, and managing the conflict (Meadows, Doster, and Jackson 2000). These religious conflicts often affect how teachers approach their science teaching, as some teachers avoid controversial content altogether or even teach religious views (Berkman and Plutzer 2011). Preservice teachers who reported personal conflicts between science and religion have shown less sophisticated NOS views, less evolution understanding, and higher preferences for students to learn, and believe in, creationism in schools (Nehm, Kim, and Sheppard 2009). Importantly, it was the perception of science-religion conflict, not religiosity, that mattered most for these preservice teacher preferences (Nehm, Kim, and Sheppard 2009).

Preservice science teachers who perceive science-religion conflicts may actively not learn evolution content, skillfully avoid expressing anti-evolution views in coursework, and repurpose evolution-teaching activities and vocabulary to match their own worldviews during instruction (Larkin and Perry-Ryder 2015). A few years ago, I had a preservice teacher in my methods course who embodied this skillful resistance. She completed her required evolution coursework, articulated her role as champion of standards-based evolution content, and successfully completed her graduation requirements. When she obtained a science teaching job, her fellow colleagues alerted me about her propensity for sharing biblical stories in her classes and her obvious resistance toward teaching evolution. Some preservice teachers thus talk the talk in their teacher education programs, never intending to walk the walk in their future classrooms.

Even preservice science teachers who personally maintain that science and religion are compatible experience anxiety when teaching about evolution and other science content that may be perceived as conflicting with students' religious views. In general, preservice science teachers are very nervous about teaching particular topics that contradict literal biblical accounts. I interview my students about topics that they believe will garner the most student resistance and they consistently identify topics such as evolution and the Big Bang (Borgerding and Dagistan 2018). Beyond these professional concerns, preservice teachers also have social concerns about their abilities to fulfill the expectations of various stakeholders such as teacher education faculty and peers (Balgopal 2014).

In studies examining what preservice science teachers do or say they would do when confronted with student opposition to science content based on religious objections, preservice teachers respond in several ways. In one study, I observed my preservice teachers while they taught evolution during their student teaching. These student teachers used a variety of approaches: addressing science-religion tensions explicitly, using NOS approaches to distinguish science from religion, and avoiding religion altogether (Borgerding et al. 2015). In a mock interview with a religious-objector parent, preservice teachers emphasized what counts and does not count as science, explained the nature of scientific theories, justified their teaching by referencing standards documents and high-stakes tests, and emphasized that students were to understand but not necessarily accept contested content (Dotger, Dotger, and Tillotson 2010; also see Chapter 7 for the understanding-but-not-necessarily-believing approach in middle and high schools). Preservice teachers benefit from these opportunities to reflect on potential science-religion conflicts while they are still in their teacher education programs.

RECOMMENDATIONS AND RESOURCES FOR COLLEGE FACULTY

Clearly, religion is an important consideration for those of us teaching college science classes and teacher education classes when evolution, Big Bang, geologic time, and other controversial content are being taught. At a time in their epistemological journeys when questions of authority, justification, and certainty run rampant, we faculty members have the opportunity to better serve students' needs. Below, I provide some recommendations and suggest particular resources for college science faculty and science education faculty when approaching science-religion issues in their coursework and programs.

College science faculty have a critical role in helping college science students understand the scientific validity of contested content while also doing their best to not alienate conflicted college learners. A critical challenge for college science faculty is to acknowledge their students' religious views. Students will experience college science classes differently if they sense that their personal beliefs are under attack. At the very minimum, college science faculty can help students understand what science is and how it is practiced in order to distinguish it from religion. In this regard, faculty should help students understand the bounded NOS in that science is limited to phenomena for which we can make observations and inferences and consequently is unable to investigate matters of the supernatural (Southerland and Scharmann 2013). Faculty interested in helping students develop this understanding of NOS can draw upon resources such as those made available through the Evolution and Nature of Science Institute website (found at *web.archive. org/web/20180220170105/http://www.indiana.edu:80/~ensiweb/home.html*). Its lesson entitled "How's Your Horoscope?" playfully articulates this science-pseudoscience distinction, and the "Science Is … Science Is NOT" activity explicitly demarcates science and non-science without directly invoking religion.

If college science faculty members are comfortable taking a further step to mitigate religious students' concerns, they may refer students to resources that help them understand different religious denominations' stances on science-religion issues such as the *Voices for Evolution* statements from various denominations (Sager 2008) or Martin's (2010) exhaustive chronicle of evolution positions. A science professor could direct students to the third section of *Voices* to investigate the myth that religion is necessarily resistant to evolution. Faculty may also share information about scientists who reconciled their own science-religion conflicts by recommending readings such as Kenneth Miller's (2007) *Finding Darwin's God* (see also Chapter 10). In addition, faculty members may freely share their own personal stories, if relevant, and provide private office-hour time for students to share their personal questions and challenges. To prepare themselves for these kinds of conversations, faculty may want to learn more about common creationist challenges and suggestions for addressing these arguments (Rennie 2002).

For college science teacher educators, my experience has taught me that I must reach two very different groups of preservice teachers: those who themselves have personal conflicts and the larger group who will likely face student, faculty, administrative, and parent resistance to the teaching of science topics that may be perceived to be controversial. Each year, I have several of both in my science methods classes.

Preservice science teachers have anxiety about teaching particular science content that may conflict with students' personal religious views. Science teacher education programs must help preservice science teachers recognize that science and religion conflicts represent a multicultural issue in science education (Jackson et al. 1995). In doing so, teacher educators must help preservice teachers expect and respect differences among their students. Clearly, science teacher education programs must prepare preservice teachers to teach about NOS, especially bounded NOS. The third quote that opens this chapter illustrates how one of my former preservice science teachers planned to use this approach. In this way, preservice teachers must know about resources that they can share with students for science-religion distinctions—for example, the "creation/evolution continuum" (Scott 1999), resources from the National Center for Science Education (*https://ncse.com*), and the National Science Teaching Association position statement on teaching evolution (*www.*

nsta.org/about/positions/evolution.aspx). When my preservice teachers see the wide range of positions on the creation/evolution continuum, many are instantly relieved that evolution acceptance is not an either-or decision about religion.

Furthermore, preservice science teachers need to learn about the U.S. court decisions that affect their teaching pertaining to science-religion conflicts (see Chapters 3 and 4 for more comprehensive overviews). In a survey of Minnesota biology teachers, for example, vast majorities of teachers did not realize that they could not be required to give equal time to creationism, that they do not have to modify their evolution instruction for religious rejecters, and that a school can force a teacher to teach evolution and to stop teaching religious accounts (Moore 2004). My preservice teachers often want to avoid acknowledging religion at all in their classes and they are relieved to learn that laws support them explicitly distinguishing science from non-science. Vaughn and Robbins (2017) found that an essay assignment requiring preservice science teachers to explain why evolution should be taught and why creationism cannot be taught was particularly influential.

> *"The act of characterizing science as an empirically driven and tentative but robust, essentially human enterprise can be used to prompt college learners' epistemological growth."*

More broadly, science teacher educators must provide preservice teachers with tools for teaching controversial issues: rationales for teaching these topics, ways to communicate the expectation that students need not abandon their religious views to gain an understanding of content, and inquiry approaches to engage their students with evidence. Specific activities in methods courses may include role-playing various scenarios as suggested by Dotger, Dotger, and Tillotson (2010) and conducting interviews with science teachers about their experiences and approaches for addressing science-religion issues (Shane et al. 2016). Many of my own preservice science teachers find inquiry approaches especially helpful for teaching science as a nondogmatic endeavor.

For preservice science teachers who reject the validity of science because of their own religious views, college science teacher educators have a critical role. Science teacher educators must ensure that preservice science teachers understand that, although they personally reject evolution/Big Bang/geologic time, these topics are widely accepted within the scientific community. These preservice teachers must understand that they will be responsible for teaching and for carrying out the general missions of their state standards and the *Next Generation Science Standards* (NGSS Lead States 2013). It is also vital that these students understand the laws pertaining to the teaching of evolution (Moore 2004). Personally, I have found that my conflicted preservice science teachers take great relief when they first learn about NOS and the existence of a spectrum of positions on the relationships between science and religion. These individuals are often the most committed to helping their own future, often conflicted, students.

CONCLUSION

Religion can be useful for teaching about NOS as an enterprise. The act of characterizing science as an empirically driven and tentative but robust, essentially human enterprise can be used to prompt college learners' epistemological growth. Our college science learners are already pondering these questions, and my hope is that college science faculty and college teacher education faculty can help support them in this process.

REFERENCES

Balgopal, M. M. 2014. Learning and intending to teach evolution: Concerns of preservice biology teachers. *Research in Science Education* 44 (1): 27–52.

Barnes, M. E., and S. E. Brownell. 2016. Practices and perspectives of college instructors on addressing religious beliefs when teaching evolution. *CBE-Life Sciences Education* 15 (2): 2.

Berkman, M. B., and E. Plutzer. 2011. Defeating creationism in the courtroom, but not in the classroom. *Science* 331 (6016): 404–405.

Borgerding, L. A., and M. Dagistan. 2018. Preservice science teachers' concerns and approaches for teaching socioscientific and controversial issues. *Journal of Science Teacher Education* 29 (4): 283–306.

Borgerding, L. A., H. Deniz, and E. S. Anderson. 2017. Evolution acceptance and epistemological views of college biology students. *Journal of Research in Science Teaching* 54 (4): 493–519.

Borgerding, L. A., V. A. Klein, R. Ghosh, and A. Eibel. 2015. Student teachers' approaches to teaching biological evolution. *Journal of Science Teacher Education* 26 (4): 371–392.

Brickhouse, N. W., Z. R. Dagher, W. J. Letts, and H. L. Shipman. 2000. Diversity of students' views about evidence, theory, and the interface between science and religion in an astronomy course. *Journal of Research in Science Teaching* 37 (4): 340–362.

Dotger, S., B. H. Dotger, and J. Tillotson. 2010. Examining how preservice science teachers navigate simulated parent-teacher conversations on evolution and intelligent design. *Science Education* 94 (3): 552–570.

Ecklund, E. H., and C. P. Scheitle. 2007. Religion among academic scientists: Distinctions, disciplines, and demographics. *Social Problems* 54 (2): 289–307.

Findley, A. M., S. J. Lindsey, and S. Watts. 2001. The impact of religious belief on learning in the science classroom. Paper presented at the Annual Meeting of the Mid-South Educational Research Association, Little Rock, AR.

Hofer, B. K., and P. R. Pintrich. 1997. The development of epistemological theories: Beliefs about knowledge and knowing and their relation to learning. *Review of Educational Research* 67 (1): 88–140.

Jackson, D. F., E. C. Doster, L. Meadows, and T. Wood. 1995. Hearts and minds in the science classroom: The education of a confirmed evolutionist. *Journal of Research in Science Teaching* 32 (6): 585–611.

Larkin, D. B., and G. M. Perry-Ryder. 2015. Without the light of evolution: A case study of resistance and avoidance in learning to teach high school biology. *Science Education* 99 (3): 549–576.

Long, D. E. 2012. The politics of teaching evolution, science education standards, and *being* a creationist. *Journal of Research in Science Teaching* 49 (1): 122–139.

Loving, C. C., and A. Foster. 2000. The religion-in-the-science-classroom issue: Seeking graduate student conceptual change. *Science Education* 84 (4): 445–468.

Manwaring, K. F., J. L. Jensen, R. A. Gill, and S. M. Bybee. 2015. Influencing highly religious undergraduate perceptions of evolution: Mormons as a case study. *Evolution: Education and Outreach* 8: 23.

Martin, J. W. (2010). Compatibility of major U.S. Christian denominations with evolution. *Evolution: Education and Outreach* 3: 420–431.

Martin-Hansen, L. M. 2008. First-year college students' conflict with religion and science. *Science & Education* 17 (4): 317–357.

Meadows, L., E. Doster, and D. F. Jackson. 2000. Managing the conflict between evolution and religion. *American Biology Teacher* 62 (2): 102–107.

Miller, K. R. 2007. *Finding Darwin's God: A scientist's search for common ground between God and evolution*. New York: Harper Perennial.

Moore, R. 2004. How well do biology teachers understand the legal issues associated with the teaching of evolution? *BioScience* 54 (9): 860–865.

Nehm, R. H., S. Y. Kim, and K. Sheppard. 2009. Academic preparation in biology and advocacy for teaching evolution: Biology versus non-biology teachers. *Science Education* 93 (6): 1122–1146.

NGSS Lead States. 2013. *Next Generation Science Standards: For states, by states.* Washington, DC: National Academies Press.

Paz-y-Mino, G., and A. Espinosa. 2010. New England faculty and college students differ in their views about evolution, creationism, intelligent design, and religiosity. *Evolution: Education and Outreach* 4: 298.

Perry, W. G. 1970. *Intellectual and ethical development in the college years: A scheme.* Cambridge, MA: Harvard University Press.

Rennie, J. 2002. 15 answers to creationist nonsense. *Scientific American* 287 (1): 78–85.

Rissler, L. J., S. I. Duncan, and N. M. Caruso. 2014. The relative importance of religion and education on university students' views of evolution in the Deep South and state science standards across the United States. *Evolution: Education and Outreach* 7: 24.

Sager, C., ed. 2008. *Voices for evolution.* Berkeley, CA: National Center for Science Education.

Scott, E. 1999. The creation/evolution continuum. *Reports of the National Center for Science Education* 19: 16–23.

Shane, J. W., I. C. Binns, L. Meadows, R. S. Hermann, and M. J. Benus. 2016. Beyond evolution: Addressing broad interactions between science and religion in science teacher education. *Journal of Science Teacher Education* 27 (2): 165–181.

Shipman, H. L., N. W. Brickhouse, Z. Dagher, and W. J. Letts. 2002. Changes in student views of religion and science in a college astronomy course. *Science Education* 86 (4): 526–547.

Sinclair, A., M. P. Pendarvis, and B. Baldwin. 1997. The relationship between college zoology students' beliefs about evolutionary theory and religion. *Journal of Research and Development in Education* 30 (2): 118–125.

Smith, S. L., and R. A. Eve. 2009. Texas biology and biological anthropology faculty express their views on teaching evolution. *Evolution: Education and Outreach* 2: 181.

Southerland, S. A., and L. C. Scharmann. 2013. Acknowledging the religious beliefs students bring into the science classroom: Using the bounded nature of science. *Theory Into Practice* 52 (1): 59–65.

Stirrat, M., and R. E. Cornwell. 2013. Eminent scientists reject the supernatural: A survey of the Fellows of the Royal Society. *Evolution: Education and Outreach* 6: 33.

Torres, J. R. F. 2009. How do preservice teachers' religious beliefs affect their understanding of astronomy? *Astronomy Education Review* 7 (2): 25–39.

Vaughn, A. R., and J. R. Robbins. 2017. Preparing preservice K–8 teachers for the public school: Improving evolution attitudes, misconceptions, and legal confusion. *Journal of College Science Teaching* 47 (2): 7–15.

Winslow, M. W., J. R. Staver, and L. C. Scharmann. 2011. Evolution and personal religious belief: Christian university biology-related majors' search for reconciliation. *Journal of Research in Science Teaching* 48 (9): 1026–1049.

Lessons About Science and Religion From Informal Science Educators

Briana Pobiner, Trish Mace, and Jennifer Collins

For informal science educators in science museums and other informal learning venues, the goals for engaging visitors are similar to the goals that science teachers in more formal, classroom settings have for their students: We want them to learn, we want them to get excited about what they learn, and we want them to want to learn more. While there are both similarities and differences in how informal and formal educators approach these goals, some of the obstacles are the same, especially when it comes to challenging conversations.

Through our own work as education practitioners who train volunteers and through the research findings of others, it is evident that we have much common ground with science teachers. In this chapter, we share what we learned from studying the effectiveness of a professional development session we facilitated in December 2015, for public-facing volunteers at the Smithsonian's National Museum of Natural History (NMNH), on navigating conversations about evolution with museum visitors. We also bring to bear our combined decades' worth of experiences teaching high school science (in the case of Jennifer) and working with teachers, mainly in workshop settings focused on teaching evolution, climate change, and ocean science.

This chapter introduces information on visitor learning of evolution in informal education venues (particularly museums) and describes how we prepared volunteers at NMNH to handle visitor concerns about evolution and what the volunteers found useful from our professional development session. We then outline concrete strategies to use when facing potentially difficult interactions, with an emphasis on strategies that can also be used in the classroom. We also note some useful online resources you can access to increase your confidence in preparing for these kinds of interactions.

LEARNING ABOUT EVOLUTION IN INFORMAL EDUCATION VENUES

As most Americans spend less than 5% of their life in classrooms, there is great potential for a lot of outside-the-classroom science learning in places like museums and science centers, zoos, aquariums, national parks, and libraries, as well as during community-based activities such as 4H and scouting and from educational digital media (Falk and Dierking 2010). Most adults in the United States have at one time in their lives visited a natural history or science museum, and natural history museums receive about 50 million visitors annually (National Science Board 2006; MacFadden et al. 2007). With reference to evolution in particular, museums are one of the primary ways that both children and adults are exposed to evolution content (Spiegel et al. 2006). A study at the New York Hall of Science found that 84% of visitors said they were interested in bringing children to an exhibit on evolution, and another study at the University of Pennsylvania Museum found that nearly all participants (children and adults) were interested in attending an exhibit on human evolution (Borun 2002; Stein and Storksdieck 2005).

While science museum visitors can be thought of as a self-selected audience interested in nature and science, reasons for visiting and levels of content understanding actually vary. Studies in U.S. museums generally find that visitors are interested in learning about evolution and less likely to reject evolution than the general public, but that many of them have a limited understanding of evolutionary terms and concepts (Spiegel et al. 2006). A study characterized high school and adult visitors to six U.S. natural history museums as having an "incomplete" understanding of evolutionary concepts (MacFadden et al. 2007). For example, while the museum visitors understood that fossils represent evidence for evolution and that fossils in lower rock layers typically are older than those in higher rock layers, only 30% used natural selection as a framework to explain why the modern cheetah runs faster than its ancestor. However, another study of visitors to the *Explore Evolution* exhibit, which was on display in several regional natural history museums in the Midwestern United States, found that people who had visited museums more often, even as children, were more likely to use evolutionary terms in their explanations of change over time (Diamond and Evans 2007). Museum visitors are more likely to accept human evolution than the general public but are still more willing to accept evolution in non-human organisms than in humans, similar to studies of the U.S. adult public by organizations such as Pew and Gallup (Squire and Hubbell Mackinney 1996; Stein and Storksdieck 2005; Spiegel et al. 2006; Pobiner 2016). As with the public in general, several studies have found that education level and religiosity are predictors of an understanding of evolution among museum visitors (Pawlukiewicz, Doering, and Paasch 1990; Stein and Storksdieck 2005; Barone, Petto, and Campbell 2014).

Despite the above research, we are aware of only one study that looks at how museum exhibits with a large focus on evolution might provoke discussions about the relationship between science and religion among visitors or between educators (staff or volunteers) and visitors. In her description of a one-day training session for gallery educators at the Natural History Museum in London in anticipation of Darwin Year in 2009, Gay (2012, p. 102) noted that "it is the conversations between educators and visitors about our specimens that offer the greatest potential for stimulating interactions about evolution—

and the greatest risk of conflict or misunderstanding or offense." The educators felt they needed more support in fossil evidence and deep time, evidence for natural selection, and evolution and faith. The museum brought together a group of content experts, educators, and diversity experts to work through and develop appropriate responses to five common scenarios that would "uphold our scientific credibility and retain visitors' engagement wherever possible, giving them the evidence to come to their own conclusions" (Gay 2012, p. 102). While the author does not report any formal evaluation of the effectiveness of this training, she states that their educators encountered very little antagonism and that most visitors were eager to engage in constructive and friendly discussions and to learn more about evolution.

HELPING MUSEUM VOLUNTEERS ADDRESS EVOLUTION

At NMNH we get requests from volunteers, particularly those in the Hall of Human Origins (HHO) and the Sant Ocean Hall (SOH), for support and information on how to engage visitors in conversations about evolution and climate change, two challenging science topics. Sometimes deemed to be "controversial," these topics infuse most exhibits at the NMNH and can often be addressed with similar strategies. When one of us (Briana) led the first series of professional development sessions in 2009 for new HHO volunteers, it became very clear that many of them were anxious and worried about visitors being argumentative or combative about the potential or actual science-religion interface in the exhibit—which has an unmistakable focus on human evolution and includes climate change messages. Therefore, addressing these concerns became a necessary and welcome element of the overall HHO new-volunteer training sessions.

To further support our volunteers' needs and better understand the conversations they might be anticipating (both positively and negatively), we developed and led an additional professional development session in December 2015. This session was held twice, was open to any public-facing volunteer at NMNH, and was based in part on what was developed earlier to address needs surrounding evolution conversations in the HHO. We also included climate change because it is another focus in many of the permanent and temporary exhibits at NMNH (e.g., SOH, the Mammals Hall, and the Fossil Halls), and the National Center for Science Education (NCSE) identified it in January 2012 as a second core area of science that is accepted by the scientific community but controversial among the public (Branch 2012). In this chapter, though, we focus mainly on evolution. The 38 volunteers who participated in the sessions were from the museum's public-facing exhibits (HHO; SOH; Geology, Gems, and Minerals; Last American Dinosaur; Genome), both permanent and temporary, and from other venues including the visitor information desks, "Q?rius," "Q?rius Jr." (a discovery room), the Insect Zoo, and the Butterfly Pavilion. Their experience with volunteering ranged from less than 1 year to more than 20 years, and several were volunteering in more than one exhibit or other venue.

The main goals for the two 2-hour professional development sessions were (a) to offer volunteers opportunities to share the challenges they face when interacting with visitors about evolution and climate change; and (b) to provide volunteers strategies for dealing with visitors who challenge the veracity of, or express doubts about, evolution and/or climate change. We suspect that these are worthy goals for any science teacher or educator to consider. We organized the sessions via the following five components, aside from introductions and summary discussions. We think these components could also be useful for organizers to consider when creating professional development opportunities for teachers, and they could be adapted to support teachers in their interactions with students, parents, other teachers, and administrators.

1. *Guiding principles.* We first provided an overview of challenges commonly faced by volunteers, and the museum's general approach and philosophy for handling them, including the official statements on evolution and climate change.

2. *Brainstorming difficult situations.* As individuals, volunteers wrote down visitor statements and/or questions related to evolution or climate change that they either had found or anticipated finding challenging. Facilitators included volunteers' responses from a presurvey and sorted the questions according to emergent categories.

3. *Brainstorming possible solutions to difficult situations.* This included whole-group discussion and presentation of strategies for productive discussions. Participants and facilitators shared effective and ineffective strategies for addressing the two topics and some of the specific questions generated previously.

4. *Role-playing scenarios.* Volunteers took on roles of visitors and volunteers to act out scenarios and practice different strategies.

5. *Receiving a list of useful resources.* Facilitators presented a list of useful websites for further exploration of evolution, climate science, and science-religion interactions.

As we describe in the next section, the professional development session was very successful overall, and it prompted many animated discussions. You might consider a similar structure with your colleagues in your school, district, or professional organization.

LESSONS FOR SCIENCE TEACHERS FROM MUSEUM PROFESSIONAL DEVELOPMENT

To gauge what components of the professional development sessions were most useful to the volunteers, we conducted three online surveys: one before the sessions, one immediately after the sessions, and one about eight months after the sessions. In the presession survey, we asked, "Describe an interaction you have had with a visitor about evolution, climate change, or another topic that you felt was challenging for you, either because it made you uncomfortable or because you felt you handled it unsuccessfully. How did the interaction begin? How did it end? Upon reflection, what might you have done differently?" While 11 of the volunteers reported that they had not had any challenging interactions, several described being questioned in ways many science teachers can identify with, including doubts about the reliability of geological dating techniques and accepting the veracity of scientific claims without actually personally conducting experiments. Echoing other challenges that classroom teachers face, the volunteers also noted that visitors expressed common misconceptions about human evolution, indicated by questions such as "If humans evolved from apes, why are there still apes?" (Johnson et al. 2012), as well as a general disbelief in evolution. However, many said that these interactions were not necessarily challenging, but often quite enjoyable and satisfying to both the volunteers and (they perceived) the visitors with whom they were interacting.

Another presession question was "What do you hope to get out of this professional enrichment?" The answers to this question made it clear that, while we designed this session to focus on interaction techniques, volunteers were also looking for more scientific content to increase their confidence in interacting with visitors; we suspect that many teachers would have similar requests. Relevant answers included "Confidence to diplomatically handle any potentially challenging situations"; "I hope to have ready responses when a visitor says that they don't 'believe in' evolution or climate change"; "How to answer a question or pointed statement without devolving into an argument or protracted discussion"; "Common questions/comments from visitors and strategies for approaching them"; and "A better understanding of the topics and to be able to better handle a difficult discussion."

Such responses accord with a survey of California science teachers at the 2000 National Conference on the Teaching of Evolution, which found that teachers wanted both more content and higher confidence levels to prepare to teach evolution (Scotchmoor and Thanukos 2007). Even teachers with very strong content knowledge and background training in the topic might feel uncertain about some aspects of evolution and feel caught off guard when asked a question they do not immediately have the information to answer. We consistently reminded the volunteers that even scientists and other content experts do not have all the answers. One way that facilitators can handle questions they are unsure of is to bring visitors along the scientific thinking journey with phrasing to engage them in the process of discovery. An example: "That's a great question! I don't know the answer, but let's think about how we might find out, or what type of evidence would help answer it." In both informal settings and classrooms, challenges can be turned to discussions of the types of investigations and evidence that could shed light on the question. In the classroom (see the other chapters in this part of the book for more targeted suggestions), these discussions can lead to student examinations of scientific literature and to providing opportunities for students to discover what evidence is documented by scientists and how this evidence was obtained.

Out of the 38 volunteers who participated in the professional development sessions, 30 reported on the immediate postsession survey that our overview of the museum's stance on topics related to evolution and climate change was very useful. In fact, this session component had the highest number of "very useful" (as opposed to "moderately useful" and "not useful") answers in the survey. The museum's press office put out an official statement about evolution on August 28, 2007 (NMNH 2007), and there are a few important elements that parallel the responsibilities of teachers, such as the following: "The National Museum of Natural History has the responsibility to share with the public the latest research on the process of evolution. It is not the museum's responsibility or intent to determine how visitors relate this information to their own religious or personal views." Like the museum, teachers' responsibilities lie in relaying the science and not negotiating the role of religion. (See Chapter 7, p. 88, for a position statement developed for a high school science department.) Additionally, the museum's statement explicitly addresses common misconceptions that teachers face, such as the following examples: "Evolution is just a theory," "Evolution is solely a product of random chance," "Humans are exempt from evolution," and "There is a scientific controversy over whether evolution occurred." Explicitly targeting misconceptions about evolution in classroom instruction is a vital opportunity for teachers as this can lead to significant gains in student understanding (Robbins and Roy 2007; Cunningham and Wescott 2009).

While we do not suggest that our volunteers carry this statement around with them in their pockets so they can read it verbatim to visitors, volunteers reported that when they became familiar with the museum's official statement, it made them feel more comfortable about what they could focus on in their engagement with visitors. Teachers may also benefit from being familiar with the evolution teaching statements of strong science education organizations. These include the National Science Teaching Association (NSTA) statement, which begins, "NSTA strongly supports the position that evolution is a major unifying concept in science and should be emphasized in K–12 science education frameworks and curricula. Furthermore, if evolution is not taught, students will not achieve the level of scientific literacy needed to be well-informed citizens and prepared for college and STEM careers" (NSTA 2013). Likewise, the National Association of Biology Teachers (NABT) position statement ends with the following: "Biological evolution must be presented in the same way that it is understood within the scientific community: as a well-accepted principle that provides the foundation to understanding the natural world. Evolution should not be misrepresented as 'controversial,' or in need of 'critical analysis' or special attention for any supposed 'strength or weakness' any more than other scientific ideas are. Biology educators at all levels must work to encourage the development of and support for standards, curricula, textbooks, and other instructional frameworks that prominently include evolution and its mechanisms and that refrain from confusing non-scientific with scientific explanations in science instruction" (NABT, 2011). If you are concerned about the legal aspects of teaching evolution, the NCSE (2000) has useful resources on that topic (also see Chapter 4 for an in-depth look at legal matters).

Out of the five aforementioned components of the professional development session, on the immediate postsession survey, volunteers scored receiving a list of useful resources with the next highest number of "very useful" responses. When brainstorming, volunteers felt uneasy about several topics pertaining to evolution: for example, the role and reliability of scientific evidence related to evolution, misunderstandings of natural selection and common ancestry, misunderstandings of scientific terminology and the process of science, a mistrust of science and scientists, and conflicts with religious perspectives and geological time. The useful list of resources we provided to volunteers to tackle these challenges included five websites or sections of websites that are also highly relevant to science teachers because they were designed for science teachers! We highly recommend "Understanding Evolution" from the University of California, Berkeley (*http:// evolution.berkeley.edu*), "Evolution" from the Public Broadcasting Service (*www.pbs.org/wgbh/ evolution*), "Evolution Resources" from the National Academy of Sciences (*www.nas.edu/ evolution/index.html*), "Evolution on the Front Line" from the American Association for the Advancement of Science (*www.aaas.org/news/evolution-front-line*), and "Evolution Education" from the National Center for Science Education (*http://ncse.com/evolution*). These resources complement the myriad others discussed in this book.

During discussion components, the two professional development sessions generated a list of ways to support positive interactions and gracefully end uncomfortable interactions. In addition to acknowledging the visitors' feelings, these included some phrases you could use when talking with students in the classroom. Some examples focus on acknowledgment or validation: "I hear you," "I respect your opinion," "That's a common misunderstanding [or] I've heard that from other people too," or "Tell me more about that." Others were phrases that bring the attention back to the science content: "I'm here to help you understand the science/research behind the exhibit," "Scientific evidence/consensus shows …," "That's a great question; let's figure out how to look for the answer," or "With the discovery of _____, we now know that … [talk about how scientific knowledge builds on itself as additional evidence is gathered]." Still others were phrases that were explicitly trying to avoid conflict: "I don't want to have an argument" and "I too have personal religious beliefs, but what I'm here to talk about is science." We encourage you to weigh this advice with the other perspectives in this book.

We were heartened to find that between the survey the volunteers took immediately after the professional enrichment and the survey they took eight months later, volunteers' confidence in engaging visitors on these subjects increased! On a scale of 1 to 5, with 1 being extremely confident and 5 being not at all confident, 70% of volunteers chose 1 or 2 and 11% chose 5 immediately after the session. That shifted to 80% choosing 1 or 2 and none of them choosing 5 eight months later. While we cannot pinpoint the reason for this increase, informal conversations we have had with some of the volunteers suggest it is related to the volunteers using the strategies they learned.

ADDITIONAL RESOURCES AND RECOMMENDATIONS FOR SCIENCE TEACHERS

We recognize that museum settings are both similar to and different from formal classroom settings. The purpose of this chapter is not to review how evolution is most effectively communicated in informal settings as a way to enhance teachers' ability to do the same in the classroom, although there is ample research on that topic. Other resources (including many we mention above) focus on best practices in teaching evolution. Here we focus instead on applicable lessons to be learned from the experiences of museum volunteers who might face challenging conversations about evolution, much like teachers. For instance, there is a sense of confidence that can be gained by becoming familiar with the official statements on evolution from NSTA and NABT that we referred to earlier, in addition to those of your own school district. We also suggest seeking out professional development experiences that specifically focus on effective strategies for teaching about evolution, including group discussions and peer mentoring. Using real-world scenarios based on the challenges a teacher might face in the classroom and working with colleagues or evolution education professionals can help provide teachers, as it has done with our volunteers, with strategies for responding to questions or resistant statements. In fact, coming up with strategies for productive discussions was the most used component of the professional development session, with 70% of volunteers reporting that they used one of the approaches we brainstormed when interacting with visitors.

Numerous studies have demonstrated that students' religiosity is probably the strongest factor conditioning their acceptance of evolution and that students are likely to be reluctant to learn evolution if they even perceive a conflict with their religious beliefs (Pobiner 2016). If you are ready to devote classroom time to activities to help reduce students' conflict between evolution and religion, a few recent studies have described such activities and demonstrated their effectiveness. Barnes, Elser, and Brownell (2017) outlined how including a discussion of the compatibility of evolution and religion into a two-week module about evolution in an introductory biology course for undergraduate majors reduced the number of students who perceived a conflict between evolution and religion by 53%. This included both religious and nonreligious students. A follow-up study by the same researchers with the same student population demonstrated that even six minutes of instruction illustrating the potential compatibility of religion and evolution reduced the level of perceived conflict in 8 out of 10 of the students they gathered data on who felt conflicted before the evolution module (Truong, Barnes, and Brownell 2018). They identified distinct aspects of the evolution instruction that the students stated reduced their level of perceived conflict, which any teacher can do in the classroom, such as not forcing student acceptance of evolution, being respectful of students with multiple viewpoints on evolution, and providing a broad exposure to evolution content.

In a study of high school Advanced Placement biology classes in 10 schools in 8 states where teachers used human case studies to teach evolution (NMNH 2018), Pobiner et al. (2018) demonstrated that using either one of two "cultural and religious sensitivity" activities led to higher increases in student understanding of evolution. In one activity, students explored the nature of science and possible relations between science

> *"While museum volunteers usually have only a single, brief opportunity to engage visitors about evolution, teachers have the advantage of an extended period of time over the school year, with repeated interactions not only to layer and scaffold content knowledge but also to build trust with students."*

and religious or cultural beliefs. In the other, students drafted both historical and modern-day responses to concerns about evolution highlighted by eight historical characters from when Charles Darwin's *On the Origin of Species* was published. These two activities are available for your use at the NMNH website (*http://humanorigins.si.edu/education/teaching-evolution-through-human-examples*).

While museum volunteers usually have only a single, brief opportunity to engage visitors about evolution (the average museum visitor spends about 20 minutes in an exhibition, as shown in Serrell 1998), teachers have the advantage of an extended period of time over the school year, with repeated interactions not only to layer and scaffold content knowledge but also to build trust with students. Communicator credibility requires both expertise and trustworthiness, and recent research demonstrates that teachers are rated as both competent and warm in relation to people who hold other jobs (Fiske and Dupree 2014). This level of trust that your students place in you provides opportunities, but it also comes with responsibilities. As communicators of evolution, it is also important for teachers to use clear and careful language when teaching the topic, particularly because many everyday words often have different meanings when used in a scientific context. Some examples related to evolution include *adaptation*, *fitness*, *selection*, *competition*, *pressure*, and *theory* (see Pobiner 2016). Imprecise, vague, confusing, and anthropomorphic communication about evolution can lead to reinforcement of misconceptions; taking the time to model and distinguish multiple meanings of terms used in scientific versus everyday contexts in the classroom is critical (Rector, Nehm, and Pearl 2013).

We encourage our volunteers to try to discern where a visitor's question comes from; if it is a misconception about evolution, simply presenting accurate information—while a good place to start—may not be enough to correct the misconception (Cunningham and Wescott 2009). Instead, the misconception must be made explicit and then the person with the misconception must decide for himself or herself that it is inaccurate. You can gently guide your students on this kind of journey, offering reassurance and encouragement along the way. The "Understanding Evolution" website (*http://evolution.berkeley.edu*) includes a great list of misconceptions and how to correct them. Petto's (2005) short, online article "Why Teach Evolution?" also outlines some of the more common arguments against teaching evolution and how to counter them.

CONCLUSION

Teaching evolution can be challenging whether you are a formal or informal educator, but there are strategies and opportunities that can help any educator improve his or her ability to respond nimbly and effectively when challenges arise. At the heart of this is finding ways to increase your own content knowledge about evolution, but you also can seek out formal and informal opportunities to learn and practice strategies and skills for how to have thoughtful, supportive conversations about evolution and, when necessary, science-religion interactions with your students.

ACKNOWLEDGMENT

Data were gathered from NMNH volunteers with permission from the Smithsonian Institution's Internal Review Board, protocol HS16009, granted on December 2, 2015.

REFERENCES

Barnes, M. E., J. Elser, and S. E. Brownell. 2017. Impact of a short evolution module on students' perceived conflict between religion and evolution. *American Biology Teacher* 79 (2): 104–111.

Barone, L. M., A. J. Petto, and B. C. Campbell. 2014. Predictors of evolution acceptance in a museum population. *Evolution: Education and Outreach* 7: 23. *https://doi.org/10.1186/s12052-014-0023-2*.

Borun, M. 2002. *Being human: A design in process, four focus groups*. Philadelphia: University of Pennsylvania Museum, Museum Solutions.

Branch, G. 2012. NCSE's climate change initiative launched. *https://ncse.com/news/2012/01/ncses-climate-change-initiative-launched-0013841*.

Cunningham, D., and D. Wescott. 2009. Still more "fancy" and "myth" than "fact" in students' conceptions of evolution. *Evolution: Education and Outreach* 2: 505–517.

Diamond, J., and E. M. Evans. 2007. Museums teach evolution. *Evolution* 61 (6): 1500–1506.

Falk, J. H., and L. D. Dierking. 2010. The 95 percent solution: School is not where most Americans learn most of their science. *American Scientist* 98 (6): 486–493.

Fiske, S. T., and C. Dupree. 2014. Gaining trust as well as respect in communicating to motivated audiences about science topics. *Proceedings of the National Academy of Sciences* 111 (Supp. 4): 13593–13597.

Gay, H. 2012. Talking about evolution in natural history museums. *Evolution: Education and Outreach* 5: 101–103.

Johnson, N. A., J. J. Smith, B. Pobiner, and C. Schrein. 2012. Why are chimps still chimps? *American Biology Teacher* 74 (2): 74–80.

MacFadden, B. J., B. A. Dunckel, S. Ellis, L. D. Dierking, L. Abraham-Silver, J. Kisiel, and J. Koke. 2007. Natural history museum visitors' understanding of evolution. *BioScience* 57 (10): 875–882.

National Association of Biology Teachers (NABT). 2011. NABT position statement on teaching evolution. *https://nabt.org/Position-Statements-NABT-Position-Statement-on-Teaching-Evolution*.

National Center for Science Education (NCSE). 2000. Cans and can'ts of teaching evolution. *https://ncse.com/library-resource/cans-cants-teaching-evolution*.

National Museum of Natural History (NMNH). 2007. The process of evolution: Statement of scientific understanding. *https://web.archive.org/web/20181024183546/https:/naturalhistory.si.edu/press_office/statements/evolution.htm*.

National Museum of Natural History (NMNH). 2018. Teaching evolution through human examples. *https://humanorigins.si.edu/education/teaching-evolution-through-human-examples*.

National Science Board. 2006. *Science and engineering indicators 2006*. Arlington, TX: National Science Foundation.

National Science Teaching Association (NSTA). 2013. NSTA position statement: The teaching of evolution. *www.nsta.org/about/positions/evolution.aspx*.

Pawlukiewicz, J. D., Z. Doering, and K. Paasch. 1990. Views from the audience: Planning a new exhibition on human evolution. *Current Trends in Audience Research and Evaluation* [Papers presented at a poster session]. American Alliance of Museums, Visitor Research and Evaluation Committee, Washington, DC.

Petto, A. 2005. Why teach evolution? *https://ncse.com/library-resource/why-teach-evolution*.

Pobiner, B. 2016. Accepting, understanding, teaching, and learning (human) evolution: Obstacles and opportunities. *American Journal of Physical Anthropology* 159 (S62): 232–274.

Pobiner, B., P. Beardsley, C. Bertka, and W. Watson. 2018. Using human case studies to teach evolution in high school A.P. biology classrooms. *Evolution: Education and Outreach* 11: 3. *https://doi.org/10.1186/s12052-018-0077-7*.

Rector, M. A., R. H. Nehm, and D. Pearl. 2013. Learning the language of evolution: Lexical ambiguity and word meaning in student explanations. *Research in Science Education* 43 (3): 1107–1133.

Robbins, J. R., and P. Roy. 2007. The natural selection: Identifying and correcting non-science student preconceptions through an inquiry-based, critical approach to evolution. *American Biology Teacher* 69 (8): 460–466.

Scotchmoor, J., and A. Thanukos. 2007. Building an understanding of evolution: An online resource for teaching and learning. *McGill Journal of Education* 42 (2): 225–243.

Serrell, B. 1998. *Paying attention: Visitors and museum exhibitions.* Washington, DC: American Alliance of Museums.

Spiegel, A. N., E. M. Evans, W. Gram, and J. Diamond. 2006. Museum visitors' understanding of evolution. *Museums and Social Issues* 1 (1): 69–86.

Squire, J., and L. Hubbell Mackinney. 1996. *Learning from Lucy: What visitors want to know about human evolution.* An evaluation study of the Lucy skeleton in the "Creatures of the Ice Age" exhibit at the California Academy of Sciences. San Francisco: California Academy of Sciences.

Stein, J. K., and M. Storksdieck. 2005. *Life changes visitor museum survey: Summary of results.* Annapolis, MD: Institute for Learning Innovation.

Truong, J. M., M. E. Barnes, and S. E. Brownell. 2018. Can six minutes of culturally competent evolution education reduce students' level of perceived conflict between evolution and religion? *American Biology Teacher* 80 (2): 106–115.

PART III

Beyond the Classroom

Talking About Science and Religion
Beyond the Classroom

Joseph W. Shane

As you have progressed in this book, the authors hope that you have both broadened your own perspective about relationships between science and religion and gleaned some practical advice for your particular circumstances. We all want to continually become better science educators, and it should be clear that science-religion interactions play a significant role in this trajectory.

We now ask you to consider something that is definitely challenging, possibly daunting, and maybe a bit terrifying for some of you. What would it take for you to step outside the comfort zone of your classroom, laboratory, or science education center to engage audiences other than your students? This could include churches (possibly yours) or other faith-based organizations, school boards, legislators, or members of the community who decide to show up to a presentation or panel discussion at the local public library. The venues are available and the interest is definitely there! All that is required are committed and courageous science educators like you to step into those spaces as advocates.

For me, for example, this beyond-the-classroom work began when the pastor at my church asked me to teach a three-session adult Sunday school class. As with any class we teach for the first time, I stumbled through it. He encouraged me to keep going, and I have since taught short courses and given presentations at many regional churches and my local public library. I also teach a semester course on science and religion at my university as part of the honors program (Shane 2019). The vast majority of this advocacy work has gone really well. A few encounters, however, did not go as planned. In 2013, for example, I met with my state representative to discuss an "academic freedom" bill he was sponsoring to allow teachers to use materials to question evolution, climate change, and other established scientific ideas (see Chapter 3 for the history behind bills like these). The bill did not proceed beyond committee, but the encounter itself was rather frustrating and discouraging because he showed no interest in science or the history of efforts to undermine science in America's public school classrooms.

One take-home message I have learned is, like with our students, misgivings about science and science-religion relationships within the general population are often rooted in basic misunderstandings of certain science concepts, the nature of science itself, and the extent to which science can and should inform our decisions. This insight points to the importance of advocacy. Each of us can (and we assert should) expand our roles to become more effective and respected science educators, community members, and science-religion boundary pioneers.

The bulk of this chapter is different in format from others in the book. It is devoted to responses by four key individuals to a common set of questions about advocacy. Think of it as a kind of panel discussion. Each of our panelists was directly involved in the *Kitzmiller v. Dover Area School District* trial from 2004 to 2005 that you read about in previous chapters (Chapters 3 and 4 in particular). Because this is one of the recent pivotal science-religion events, their advice is both powerful and timeless. We then offer some additional insight about advocacy adapted from two well-known organizations, the National Science Teaching Association (NSTA) and the National Center for Science Education (NCSE), both of which engage the public as part of their mission.

GETTING MOTIVATED FOR ADVOCACY: ADVICE FROM COLLEAGUES ASSOCIATED WITH *KITZMILLER*

Jennifer Miller and Robert Eshbach are current science teachers at Dover Area High School in Pennsylvania. Ken Miller, a biologist from Brown University, is a national leader in evolution education and played an important role in explaining the science behind evolution to Judge John E. Jones III during the *Kitzmiller* trial. Eric Rothschild, of Americans United for Separation of Church and State, was one of the attorneys who represented the parents in the *Kitzmiller* case. We asked them a common set of questions about advocacy and their responses are on the next several pages.

1. Why and how did you become involved with science-religion issues? What is your story?

Jennifer Miller and Robert Eshbach: "We became involved in science-religion issues when the Dover Area School Board of Directors voted to include intelligent design in our biology curriculum in 2004. As professional educators, we opposed the inclusion of intelligent design because it is not science and, thus, it goes against our professional code of ethics. We quickly became embroiled in the *Kitzmiller* court case as witnesses."

Ken Miller: "My involvement came about for the simplest of reasons. I went into science as a career and was surprised to discover that for certain people this raised the issue of how a scientist could possibly be a person of faith. This was not a question I encountered in college, grad school, or even as a research scientist. However, it did come up in teaching. During my first year on the faculty at Brown University, I was challenged by a group of students to debate a well-known scientific creationist who was coming to campus for a lecture. This was Dr. Henry Morris, founder of the Institute for Creation Research, and our debate in April 1981 drew nearly 2,000 people to hear us debate issues of evolution and creation. I quickly learned that hostility to religion on the part of a scientist like me was assumed by both Dr. Morris and a large part of the crowd. Being a practicing, though far from perfect, Roman Catholic, I quickly rejected the stereotype he had prepared for me, and he reacted with surprise. It clearly affected the course of our discussions and disarmed some of his most emotional arguments against evolution.

"I knew very well that many mainstream Christian denominations had long since reconciled themselves to the science of evolution and was quick to point this out. But the persistent stereotype of the religion-hating scientist seemed to follow me every time I spoke publicly in defense of evolution, which I had frequent occasion to do in the contentious atmosphere of the 1980s, when the teaching of evolution seemed to be under attack from all sides. I found it important to highlight my own faith for two reasons: first, to deprive the anti-evolution movement of its automatic claim to the allegiance of all Christians, which I regarded as a gross distortion of our faith; and second, to defend science against the claim that its primary agenda is anti-religious rather than pro-knowledge. As a result, I found myself frequently invited to speak and write on this issue, and eventually it became the topic of my book *Finding Darwin's God: A Scientist's Search for Common Ground Between God and Evolution*."

Eric Rothschild: "My involvement with *Kitzmiller*, one of the great science-religion cases in the country's history, began approximately five years prior when, as a young lawyer practicing at a Philadelphia law firm, I reached out to the National Center for Science Education to see if they needed any help with their advocacy against a law in Kansas that would have barred teaching about evolution. At that time, I had no expectation that I would actually get to try a case like *Kitzmiller*—I just wanted to volunteer my interest in constitutional law and my experience with science-related cases to an organization that was doing public advocacy on this topic.

"But when the first case on the issue of teaching intelligent design as science surfaced not in Kansas, but in Pennsylvania where I was practicing, I was a more seasoned attorney and myself and my colleagues were up for the challenge. We worked with the parents who brought the lawsuit, and scientists and other experts, to persuade the court that intelligent design was religion, not science, that violated the Constitution and hurt children's education."

2. Why is it important for science educators to talk about science and religion with groups other than students? Why bother? Why not just keep the classroom door shut?

Jennifer Miller and Robert Eshbach: "Education in any area goes beyond the classroom door. Many of our students come into our classrooms with preconceived notions or ideas in

> "Science is our future, and for the United States to remain the world leader in science and technology, we need science education to open the gates of discovery to our students."

regards to science versus religion because of their upbringing. The more we are able to show that there is no controversy between science and religion, the more prepared our students will be for the classroom. As children of ministers, it is important for us to promote the idea of science and religion, not science versus religion."

Ken Miller: "It would be fine to keep the door shut if there were no one pounding on it from the outside seeking to dictate what happens in the science classroom. For better or for worse, education in the United States remains a public enterprise, subject to public opinion and requiring the support of voters. Critics of mainstream science—and there are plenty of them—understand that public education can be a powerful force in shaping the opinions of rising generations, and they desperately want the schools to endorse their own agendas, political, religious, and economic.

"That is why educators must be willing to explain to their communities what takes place in the science classroom and why it matters to them. Science is our future, and for the United States to remain the world leader in science and technology, we need science education to open the gates of discovery to our students. Pressures to twist, restrict, and distort science would ultimately stifle the scientific enterprise, as they have in every society in which science has been co-opted for political or religious purposes. This is what educators must make clear to their friends and neighbors. There is no calling greater than that of a teacher, and letting the general public see firsthand the dedication and professionalism of educators in their own cities and towns will ultimately provide the support we need for effective science education."

Eric Rothschild: "There is no good reason for science and religion to be in conflict. Many scientists and science teachers are religious, including teachers at Dover High School where the *Kitzmiller* case arose, and most faiths have no theological quarrel with the findings of modern science. But if the science community and educators stay silent on this topic, it cedes the field to the loud voices that do promote conflict. Most science educators know how to sensitively treat this subject, because of long experience educating students from a variety of faith backgrounds. And they have the credibility that comes from having selected a profession that puts children's interests first."

3. What advice do you have for talking about science and religion with fellow teachers, administrators, and school board members? How about local, state, and national legislators and policymakers?

Jennifer Miller and Robert Eshbach: "The first step is to listen to these groups to hear their opinions, with the realization that in many cases nothing that is said in support of science will change their minds. When there is an impasse, you must remind this group that a teacher's job is to teach science, not a belief, a position that has been upheld in the court system. At some point you will have no choice but to stand firmly against instituting policies that go against your professional ethics and scientific pedagogy. By the way, now would be a good time to start documenting every meeting!"

Ken Miller: "My first advice is to be candid. To be an advocate on these issues it is not necessary to be a person of faith or to pretend to be. If an educator is not religious, even if one's own views are secular to the point of atheism or agnosticism, there still is no need to pretend otherwise. The best advice I can offer for talking about science is for an educator to reveal their own passion for the subject—to be very clear why they went into science and why they became an educator. Your colleagues will quickly come to see that it was not a political or anti-religious agenda that drew you to science, but a passion for understanding and the desire to share that passion with young people. I often tell my colleagues and teaching assistants that I approach my own classes with a very simple goal in mind. I want to convince each and every one of my students that biology is very simply the coolest, most interesting, most important subject they have ever studied. And if we let others see that as our primary motivation, the other issues will take care of themselves.

"Many people in public office have established entrenched positions on certain issues and therefore are reluctant to make fundamental changes to their public stances on controversial issues. On several occasions where I have had the public or private opportunity to interact with such officeholders, I have taken care not to be directly critical of their past positions, votes, or public statements. Rather, I have attempted to make them look forward to how tomorrow's students will be educated, to the role that science will play in assuring a prosperous and secure future, and to the goal that I share with them of securing the best possible education for our young people. What I have tried to do is to position myself and the ideas I represent as a goal that we can share and work toward together rather than seeking conflict in areas where we might disagree.

"Now, I would be the first to admit that this approach does not always work. Some people simply cannot be won over, and many feel they must answer to constituencies that value political, religious, or economic special interests above the goal of comprehensive, high-quality science education. What you may be able to do, however, is to convince such officeholders of your fundamental good will, and in my own experience that often blunts some of the hostility they express toward science."

Eric Rothschild: "First and foremost, educators should communicate that their goal is not to get students to believe in scientific principles as unshakeable articles of faith, much less persuade students to discard the religious beliefs they come to school with. A teacher's job is to make sure that the students understand what scientific investigation has demonstrated—how the natural world works, what are the consequences of those natural phenomena and operations, etc. Where students take that information relative to their faith or other commitments will be up to them, but the students should be armed with the best information and comprehension that their teachers can provide them.

"Educators should also feel comfortable communicating that they cannot take sides on religious issues—the Constitution forbids this. Sticking to the science is good pedagogy, and also legally required. Nobody wants teachers to trespass constitutional boundaries that results in an expensive lawsuit.

"A lot of the messages that apply to the education community also make sense for policymakers. And policymakers should also understand that undermining science education for the purpose of endorsing certain religious positions is not just a recipe for getting sued, but hurts their communities by producing less educated students, demoralizing teachers, and incentivizing productive businesses to put down stakes in places where they can find a workforce better prepared for the modern economy."

4. How should science teachers respond if there is a really negative reaction?

Jennifer Miller and Robert Eshbach: "Teachers should search for outside resources like NCSE that have experience dealing with challenges to the scientific community. Do not feel as though you stand alone in your conflict. Colleagues in the scientific profession will be there to stand by your side."

Ken Miller: "The best response is to take seriously your role as a citizen and a member of the community. Time and time again we have seen the power of well-organized citizens for science organizations in states as diverse as Kansas, Texas, and Florida to drive change for the better. Contact your own state legislators, school board members, or public officials to let them know, personally, how important this issue is to you and to your colleagues. Teachers are respected members of the community, and they can build from that base of support to form an effective electoral movement to redirect public policy.

"I can think of no better example than the school board election that took place during the *Kitzmiller* trial in Dover, Pennsylvania, in 2005. Outraged by the manner in which the board majority had attempted to insert intelligent design into the school curriculum, a group of residents formed an organization called 'Dover Cares' and nominated a slate of pro-science candidates to run against the incumbent board. They raised money, posted signs, printed T-shirts, and went door to door soliciting votes for their candidates. On election day, every one of the incumbent board members was voted out of office, and the new board promptly rescinded the intelligent design initiative. The *New York Times* hailed the election as 'decisive,' and conservative columnist Charles Krauthammer, citing Newton and Einstein, wrote that the town of Dover had 'distinguished itself' by standing up for science at the ballot box. We should always remember that in a democracy, the ballot is our ultimate remedy, and we should never be shy about using it."

Eric Rothschild: "I watched this happen in real time in Dover. The science teachers worked tirelessly to explain to hostile board members and administrators that they were teaching evolution properly and without demeaning religion whatsoever. Despite those efforts, they were bullied, intimidated, and ultimately ignored by the board, which required teaching intelligent design even though the teachers had told the board it was not science. At that point, the teachers' recourse was with their labor union, which really stood with them, and with their own moral and professional standards. The Dover teachers refused to teach intelligent design as science because they knew it was not. That took a lot of bravery—but the result was, when the case was over, they could stand proud as professionals that they never compromised their professional standards or misled their students."

5. What is the potential and positive impact that all of this science and religion advocacy work might have?

Jennifer Miller and Robert Eshbach: "The main objective of our continued advocacy of science and religion is that these two areas of study can coexist and not be seen as an either-or scenario. Another positive impact is that advocacy forces you as the educator to stay abreast of current topics that may become controversial."

Ken Miller: "I think we are already seeing a positive impact nationwide. A 2017 Gallup poll showed that creationist belief in the United States had reached a historic low at 38%, with a majority of Americans now agreeing that human beings had indeed been produced by evolution. In addition, a 2015 Pew Foundation survey showed that 73% of Americans in the 18–29 age group accepted evolution, by far the highest percentage for any demographic group. This suggests that recently educated Americans are getting the message, and that efforts to improve and enhance science education in our schools are working. We should keep up the pressure!

"The ultimate goal of this sort of advocacy is to develop respect. It is vital that our society cultivate and encourage respect for science among all our citizens, religious and nonreligious alike. In order to do this, we must continue to work to break down the stereotypical hostility that has all too often pushed public discourse toward an attitude where science and religion are portrayed as polar opposites. The reality is that Western science was born in a religious context, was nurtured by religious institutions, and remains one of the great achievements of our culture. We must all work to ensure that this continues to be true."

Eric Rothschild: "Resolving difficult social-cultural issues through litigation—while sometimes necessary—is difficult. Communication and persuasion that result in good science education occurring, while respecting the place religious belief holds in many students' private lives, is the ideal mechanism for good science education and religious faith to exist in harmony.

"So it is important for science educators and religious leaders to speak up about these issues in the communities that trust them. It is also valuable for important public figures— including scientists, religious figures, and politicians—to be out in the public square about these issues."

GOING FURTHER INTO ADVOCACY WITH NSTA AND NCSE

NSTA is our primary national science education organization. NSTA's Communication, Legislative, and Public Affairs (CLPA) team centers on political advocacy by, for example, supporting the adoption and implementation of state- and national-level science education policies. It is instrumental in coordinating various professional organizations and mobilizing science teachers at all levels. If your needs and interests overlap with political advocacy work, take a look at the CLPA website (*www.nsta.org/about/clpa*), review an excellent article by a CLPA assistant executive director (Peterson 2011), and contact colleagues at your state-level NSTA affiliate.

NCSE (*www.ncse.com*) promotes the responsible teaching of evolution and climate science and is a vital watchdog group that helps push back against attacks on science education. It was heavily involved in the *Kitzmiller* trial. If you remember one thing from this chapter, it is that you can rely on NCSE if you run into opposition, religiously motivated or otherwise, on how you are teaching science. The NCSE website has plenty of resources for taking action: lists of do's and don'ts, webinars, letter writing, tips for organizing, media relations, and more.

In summary, here is a consolidated and modified list of advice (Figure 10.1) that we find particularly helpful for science-religion outreach. Many of the points are similar to what we already do as science teachers and educators, but with a few caveats.

Figure 10.1 is hardly an exhaustive list, and it should complement much of the advice that previous authors have provided throughout this book. To reiterate an overarching point, we need more individuals willing to develop the knowledge, perspective, patience, and compassion to traverse the boundaries between science and religion. Engaging these issues with our specific students in our own classrooms is enormously important. As your comfort level increases, we urge you to take that first step outside your classroom and add your voice to the other advocates at work for quality science teaching.

Figure 10.1. Some tips for your science-religion outreach

- *Form a broad, local coalition.* No individual can speak to every nuance of science-religion interactions, and your influence will be greater if you include a range of colleagues, parents, community members, students, and clergy who are conversant in science. You do not want to be perceived as a lone crusader with an axe to grind. Your state-level NSTA affiliate would be a good place to begin.

- *Whenever possible, get ahead of it.* If you hear, for example, a drumbeat building against the *Next Generation Science Standards*, or if a local school board member questions the adoption of certain books, use this as an opportunity to teach and inform. This may prevent a lot of unnecessary, and possibly unconstitutional and illegal, actions later on.

- *Prepare and respond, but do not debate or denigrate.* Preparing is standard stuff for a science teacher, but keep in mind that you may not know your audience in advance and some may not consider you as either an authority figure or an expert. As you have read throughout this book, evolution and other science concepts sometimes conflict with people's core identity. Know and explain the science. Understand and empathize with the range of reactions, but avoid open and hostile debates. They are not useful and they will impede your efforts.

- *Document.* This is important if you encounter potentially unconstitutional activity, but it is also useful for you as you continue in your science-religion outreach. Think of this as the lesson-plan notes for next year.

- *Tell your story and find common ground.* Putting faces with the facts is always helpful and there is likely to be broad agreement with regards to quality education, environmental stewardship, job prospects for students, and basic human dignity. We as science educators may not be comfortable with this aspect of science-religion outreach, but it is essential in our view.

REFERENCES

Peterson, J. 2011. How can science educators influence legislation at the state and federal levels? In *The role of public policy in K–12 science education*, ed. G. E. DeBoer, 241. Charlotte, NC: Information Age Publishing.

Shane, J. W. 2019. An evolving interdisciplinary seminar on science and religion. *Honors in Practice* 15: 79–94.

Promoting Dialogue on Science, Ethics, and Religion Through the American Association for the Advancement of Science

Robert O'Malley, Curtis L. Baxter III, Christine DiPasquale,
Se Kim, and Jennifer J. Wiseman

The American Association for the Advancement of Science (AAAS), founded in 1848, is the largest general science organization in the world. A primary mission of AAAS is to "advance science, engineering, and innovation throughout the world for the benefit of all people" (AAAS 2018f). In addition to publishing the *Science* family of journals, AAAS sponsors a range of initiatives in science policy and advocacy, education, career support for scientists, and public engagement on science topics. Veteran science teachers may be familiar with the AAAS initiative Project 2061, which gave the science education community its seminal documents of *Science for All Americans* (AAAS 1990), *Benchmarks for Science Literacy* (AAAS 1993), and *Atlas of Science Literacy* (AAAS 2013).

Among these initiatives is the Dialogue on Science, Ethics, and Religion (DoSER) program, established in 1995 to facilitate dialogue among scientists, ethicists, and religious communities (AAAS 2018c). Science teachers may be surprised that such a prominent scientific organization has had, for nearly 25 years, a commitment to science and religion dialogue. As an organization, AAAS recognizes the important role that religion and faith play in the way many people within the United States and worldwide frame their interest, questions, and concerns about science and technology topics (Pew Research Center 2008). Through the DoSER program, AAAS recognizes that the scientific community should engage with a broad spectrum of perspectives, both to understand the cultural context within which science operates and to respond to the societal issues presented by new findings and technological developments. AAAS provides a unique forum for such engagement due to the organization's history, disciplinary breadth, and credibility across academic, commercial, educational, and policy circles.

In recent years, the DoSER program has produced resources to facilitate dialogue between scientific and religious communities, including a book exploring thoughtful intersections between evolutionary theory and Christian perspectives (Baker and Miller 2006); has hosted regular lectures at AAAS headquarters (AAAS 2018d); and has regularly organized symposia (AAAS 2018a) at the AAAS annual meeting on science topics that intersect or resonate with religion and broader societal concerns. In this chapter, however, the goal is to focus primarily on science engagement with sensitivity to cultural (and particularly religious) values and perspectives.

What is meant by science engagement? As defined by AAAS (2018h), it is "intentional, meaningful interactions that provide opportunities for mutual learning between scientists and members of the public." Such a definition implies, among other things, a willingness to (a) consider diverse perspectives (including those of non-scientists) on a topic or issue; (b) address benefits, potential limits, and perils of scientific research and technology; (c) inform conversations with scientific evidence; and (d) be responsive to societal issues and concerns. In this chapter, several of the DoSER program's recent projects are outlined as examples of how scientists or science educators—whether persons of faith or not—and scientific or educational institutions can participate in substantive science engagement with religious individuals, institutions, and communities. Critically, our program recognizes that there is no monolithic "public" but rather diverse publics, made up of individuals holding a wide range of concerns, values, and priorities. The chapter concludes with an overview of how the lessons we have learned can be applied by science teachers to their classrooms.

PERCEPTIONS PROJECT (2012–2015)

In 2012, the DoSER program launched the Perceptions project (AAAS 2015a) to explore and discuss conceptions (and misconceptions) that can hinder interactions between religious and scientific communities. The project included a national survey, a series of professionally facilitated workshops, and a national conference for scientists, science communicators, and religious leaders to help participants recognize stereotypes present within each community about the other. Participants were encouraged to find areas of common ground and examine the potential for dialogue about science topics (even contentious topics) grounded in genuine human relationships. The project involved four religious groups representing large U.S. constituencies that would provide useful insights for broader application—Catholics, mainline Protestants, Jews, and evangelical Christians— but primarily focused on evangelical communities as these constitute as much as 30% of the U.S. population (Pew Research Center 2008).

Participants in an early project advisory meeting—including scientists, sociologists, science advocates, and religious leaders—concluded that scientists' concerns about religious publics centered around potential interference with scientific research and education on issues such as human embryonic stem-cell research, biological evolution (especially human evolution), and climate change. Some shared interests and values were also identified, such as "investing in medical missions and the dissemination of health information and resources." Religious communities' wariness about science, as presented by National Association of Evangelicals President Leith Anderson, was centered on "how [the scientific establishment] works and what scientists believe" (AAAS 2015a).

As part of the project, AAAS and sociologists led by Elaine Howard Ecklund of Rice University conducted a survey of nearly 10,000 Americans (including rank-and-file scientists) to examine perceptions about scientists and science. Among other findings, the survey found that evangelicals consult scientists about scientific questions at rates equal to the general public (14%) but are more than twice as likely as other respondents to look to a religious leader for answers to such questions (10% vs. 4%). While evangelicals were more than twice as likely as other respondents (29% vs. 14%) to agree that "science and religion are in conflict and I am on the side of religion," 48% of evangelicals and 38% of other respondents said that science and religion can work in collaboration. Notably, more than half of evangelical scientists (57%) agreed that "most scientists are hostile to religion," whereas only 37% of other evangelicals and 24% of all scientists agreed with this statement (AAAS 2015a). Thoughtful exploration of these findings and the perceptions that underlie them guided the rest of the project. For those interested in a deeper investigation of this topic, Dr. Ecklund's extensive work on the perceptions of scientists and religious people toward each other is more thoroughly explored in two recent books:

A facilitated discussion between scientists and religious leaders as part of a DoSER Perceptions workshop

Dr. Maithilee Kunda speaking at the 2017 DoSER Holiday Lecture "Of Minds and Machines"

Science vs. Religion: What Scientists Really Think (Ecklund 2010) and *Religion vs. Science: What Religious People Really Think* (Ecklund and Scheitle 2017).

Building on the survey findings and early focus group discussions, the DoSER program hosted six community workshops in several cities across the country, each convening up to 30 scientists and religious leaders to explore issues of mutual interest and concern.

Geneticist and ordained priest Dr. Nicanor Austriaco speaking at DoSER's "Gene Editing and Human Identity" symposium at the 2018 AAAS Annual Meeting

These included discussions of a new workbook produced in collaboration with Public Agenda (a nonpartisan, nonprofit research and public engagement organization), which outlines three general approaches for dialogue—build common ground, increase collaboration, and simplify relations—that may be useful tools for facilitating discussion among students from diverse backgrounds (Public Agenda 2014).

The "Same World, Different Worldviews" workbook (downloadable at *www.aaas.org/programs/dialogue-science-ethics-and-religion/downloads*) offers a framework for productive conversation, helping participants discern answers to questions such as the following:

- What do we agree on or have in common?

- What are our important areas of disagreement—the issues we may have to keep talking about in the future?

- What are the questions and concerns that need more attention?

Beyond facilitated conversation, the workshops provided the architecture for scientists and religious leaders from the same geographical area to meet one another and spend time getting to know each other's interests and values. Brief group visits to local science labs and religious institutions were noted by several participants as very enlightening and "life-changing"; many participants were visiting spaces they had never before had the chance to enter.

Highlights and final products from the project were shared with the media and the public at a national conference in March 2015 (AAAS 2015b). (Conference video is available at *www.aaas.org/programs/dialogue-science-ethics-and-religion/video* and could be a valuable resource for sparking classroom discussion.) Beyond discussing the major themes of the project, attendees at the conference highlighted the potential role of scientists within congregations as bridge-builders and facilitators who can assist clergy and other religious leaders in dialogue about science topics. Response to the conference was overwhelmingly positive, with 79% of conference attendees reporting having left the conference with a "better understanding of the various interests and concerns of the scientific community and/or religious communities" (AAAS 2015a).

SCIENCE FOR SEMINARIES PROJECT (2014–PRESENT)

Many people of faith look to religious leaders for guidance on important issues relating to science and technology, yet clergy members often have little exposure to science in their education and training. The Science for Seminaries project was launched in 2014 as a collaboration between the AAAS-DoSER program and the Association of Theological Schools (ATS), the main accrediting body for such Christian institutions. The project goal is to provide future clergy and religious leaders with solid scientific exposure during their formal education, through coursework and regular interactions with scientists working in diverse fields. A central tenet of the ATS mission is to adequately prepare future leaders to be culturally relevant on issues faced by modern congregations, including those related to science and technology. By supporting the integration of science into the core seminary experience while leaving implementation strategies to individual seminaries, the program does not put pressure on faculty to implement new courses, but rather enables them to generate modules on science topics that can easily be integrated into existing courses and also shared with other seminaries. This integration approach gives institutions ownership of their programs while respecting different needs across a spectrum of religious traditions.

The program has garnered tremendous enthusiasm from seminaries and theological schools. Ten seminaries were selected for an initial pilot project to plan and implement revised curricula for the 2014–2016 school years. Additional courses and revisions were implemented through and beyond the original project timeline, into the spring of 2017. AAAS supported the selected institutions by recruiting curriculum planning teams drawing from theology and a spectrum of science disciplines, including astrophysics, genomics, paleontology, chemistry, neuroscience, and biology. AAAS also supported curriculum development meetings for faculty and advisory teams from each institution to meet and share ideas and resources.

As of November 2016, at least 116 courses across the 10 seminaries were affected by the pilot project. The most common science topics integrated into the curricula were neuroscience, cosmology/astronomy, and evolution. For example, Catholic University of America incorporated science content related to learning, memory, and the senses into its Foundations of Liturgy and Sacrament course. At Howard University School of Divinity, an Introduction to Hebrew Bible course integrated paleoclimatology to provide historical context for the time periods in question. Many seminaries addressed ecology and environmental sciences in ways relevant to their communities, inspired in part by Pope Francis's 2015 environmental encyclical, *Laudato Si'*. Many syllabi and other course materials generated by the project are freely available online (AAAS 2018g).

In addition to impacts in the classroom, the project supported field trips to museums and research labs, guest lectures, film screenings, book clubs, and other enrichment activities on and off campus. For example, at Wake Forest School of Divinity, students took a field trip to the Kennedy Space Center that brought one seminary leader to tears as

Science for Seminaries project seminary meeting

Dr. Georgia Dunston of Howard University being interviewed for the *Science: The Wide Angle* film series

he contemplated the magnitude and beauty of the universe. Columbia Theological Seminary students visited the Georgia Aquarium as part of an Old Testament interpretations course to better reflect on the diversity of life on Earth. These and other opportunities immersed seminarians in science while enriching their theological training and were, therefore, often warmly referred to as pilgrimage experiences by the project faculty.

The project also supported three faculty enrichment retreats in 2016 to highlight the work of each seminary and to share and disseminate ideas about how to enrich theological education within and beyond the 10 participating institutions. The retreats combined plenary presentations, field trips, and small-group discussions. Retreat participants had an opportunity to build or renew relationships with both theology colleagues and with scientists.

As a final component of the project, AAAS launched *Science: The Wide Angle* (AAAS 2016), a series of freely available, high-quality short films that feature the work of prominent researchers discussing compelling topics such as "Biological Evolution and the Kinship of All Life," "The Workings of Science," "Frontiers in Neuroscience: Charting the Complexities of Our Brains," and "Is the Human Mind Predisposed to Religious Thought?" These films are accompanied by study guides that were designed to spark classroom discussion of societal implications of the research from theological perspectives. Each film introduces science concepts or explores the nature of science, while leaving room for faculty to guide classroom discussion of societal implications and theological touch-points. Though developed for seminaries, the films are extremely accessible and useful for other postsecondary education settings as well. (The series can be viewed at *www.scienceforseminaries.org/science-the-wide-angle*, and educators can request a copy for classroom use.)

Based on the success of the initial project, Science for Seminaries Phase II was launched in late 2017. This will expand the program to at least 32 new institutions over a five-year period.

ENGAGING SCIENTISTS PROJECT (2016–PRESENT)

The Engaging Scientists in the Science and Religion Dialogue project, a collaboration between AAAS-DoSER and the AAAS Center for Public Engagement with Science and Technology, was launched in late 2016. In recent years, AAAS has fielded many questions from scientists seeking assistance in effectively engaging with religious students and publics in their classrooms and elsewhere. Specifically, scientists have sought assistance in fostering constructive dialogue about science and the societal implications of new discoveries and technological advances as well as approaches for discussing and teaching science in ways that are relevant and sensitive to a range of worldviews, belief systems, and cultural backgrounds. Accordingly, the project supports scientists in becoming more effective ambassadors for their research interests, their disciplines, and for science as a whole with a broad spectrum of publics, particularly with diverse religious communities. This project helps scientists develop strategies and skill sets for constructive and culturally competent public science engagement, especially on topics that intersect with faith and religion. The Engaging Scientists project includes four related initiatives, described as follows.

Scientific Society Events

Members of the DoSER team and facilitators from the AAAS Center for Public Engagement organized and hosted science communication workshops at prominent scientific association meetings in 2017–2018. Where appropriate, these were paired with formal research symposia highlighting effective, dialogue-driven engagement strategies and projects with religious communities and other publics that were already taking place within that discipline. Through these events, science professionals, researchers, and students gained an appreciation for cultural competence and learned strategies and best practices for science engagement with diverse audiences.

In 2017, the program hosted a social issues roundtable at the Society for Neuroscience annual meeting. A second workshop was held at the American Geophysical Union, where the program also organized a well-received poster symposium on engagement with faith communities. In 2018, workshops were held at meetings of the American Astronomical Society (featuring remarks by astronomer and science communicator Dr. Salman Hameed; AAAS 2018b), the American Society of Human Genetics (featuring remarks by geneticist Dr. Ting Wu of Harvard University), and the American Association of Physical Anthropologists (AAPA). At the AAPA, the program also organized a half-day symposium on "Dialogue with Diverse Publics," with presentations spanning paleoanthropology, primatology, genetics, forensic sciences, and public health, as well as evolution education, crowd-funding scientific research, and the 2017 March for Science. These and other presentations have been archived and are freely available online at *www.aaas.org/programs/dialogue-science-ethics-and-religion/video* (AAAS 2018e).

Campus Events

Beginning in the fall of 2018, the AAAS DoSER team and public engagement facilitators began holding science communication workshops and speaker events at U.S. research universities, geared toward both established and early-career scholars. The content focuses on effective, dialogue-driven engagement strategies for communicating about science in the classroom, in research settings, and with broader publics, in particular with religious students and audiences. Campus events have included awards to recognize and promote constructive science engagement between university scientists and their local communities, including religious institutions and publics.

Print and Online Resources

As part of the project, DoSER is producing a series of booklets (Nisbet 2018) that explore the social context for science engagement and provide an overview of best science communication practices, including for engagement with religious publics, drawing on established guidelines and the latest peer-reviewed research. The booklet series highlights science engagement projects from a range of disciplines, with commentary and reflections on these projects from lead researchers, collaborators, and participants. The project is producing an array of online resources for public engagement, including video archives of academic symposia, additional examples of science engagement projects with commentary, and web-only versions of workshops. The first booklet in the series, "Scientists in Civic Life: Facilitating Dialogue-Based Communication," can be downloaded at *www.aaas.org/programs/dialogue-science-ethics-and-religion/resources-engaging-scientists-project*.

Engaging Scientists Network

Participants in our workshops or in other DoSER activities are encouraged to join our mailing list and sign up for the "Engaging Scientists" database (*https://engagingscientists.aaas.org*), which will be a resource to link scientists interested in science advocacy and engagement activities with religious institutions and faith communities. Through online social media such as the AAAS website, Twitter, and Facebook, DoSER and its partner programs within AAAS participate in and promote dialogue on effective science engagement, share resources, and highlight opportunities for science engagement with diverse publics.

COMMON THEMES AND INSIGHTS

The DoSER program typically focuses on engagement with adults rather than with K–12 students. However, drawing on our program's experiences, especially with the projects

The AAAS-DoSER Science Communication and Engagement With Religious
Publics workshop at the 2018 Annual Meeting of the American Association
of Physical Anthropologists

outlined here, we offer the following take-home points for science teachers, educators, and communicators interested in constructive dialogue about science within and beyond the classroom, both with students and with their families.

Practice Humility

As an approach to generate and disseminate knowledge, science is an incredibly powerful tool. However, some important and fascinating questions that arise through scientific inquiry are not necessarily answerable through the tools of science alone. Science has an important role, whether it's regarding philosophical questions such as "What does it mean to be human?" or specific policy questions such as "Should humans colonize Mars?" or "How can we effectively control the spread of mosquito-borne pathogens?" But importantly, scientists are not the only voices in society with something to contribute to discussions around these questions. Furthermore, there is value in science teachers guiding their students to recognize alternative approaches to knowledge production and to nonscientific expertise, and to the important ethical concerns and boundaries regarding the uses of technology that scientists and scientific data alone cannot prescribe. Focusing on the nature of science as a tool or a process rather than a body of facts emphasizes its universality and utility for everyone.

Demonstrate Humanity

As retired AAAS CEO Alan Leshner has put it, "Scientists are people, though sometimes they pretend otherwise" (Leshner 2017). Science is ultimately a human endeavor, and framing it as such can be an incredibly useful approach to communicating science content.

For example, storytelling is an effective means to make science content personal, human, and relevant. Consider how the life story of Dr. Jane Goodall is woven into her research on wild chimpanzees in Africa, underway since 1960, and her ongoing efforts to support conservation on a global scale (Goodall 1990). Similarly, consider the social impact of the 2017 movie *Hidden Figures* (based on the book of the same name), which highlights critical contributions by Dr. Katherine Johnson, Dorothy Vaughan, and Mary Jackson, along with other African American women scientists, programmers, and engineers, to the U.S. space program (Shetterly 2016).

> **"Science is ultimately a human endeavor, and framing it as such can be an incredibly useful approach to communicating science content."**

By framing science as a story, science teachers and educators can communicate their own (or other scientists') enthusiasm about science as well as share the pitfalls, disasters, and triumphs that are normal parts of science inquiry. Stories also provide ways to illustrate how values, including those related to faith, can inform the practice of science. Stories well told are memorable and meaningful.

Seek Common Ground

While impassioned debates can be entertaining, they are not necessarily effective as a means of persuasion. In fact, extensive social science research suggests that aggressive challenges to an individual's core beliefs tend to reinforce and harden, rather than soften, opinions (Beck 2017). In contrast, dialogue provides an opportunity to explore perspectives on a topic from different frames of reference, both for scientists and others. Even when profound disagreements exist, trust can be established and solidified through meaningful personal connections, empathy, and respectful conversation. This approach can also help to identify shared values and areas of concern, and it is effective for discussions both inside and outside the science classroom. Scientific and religious communities have frequently found broad agreement and built successful collaborations on issues such as conservation and responsible stewardship of the environment (Scheller 2017), public health concerns (Centers for Disease Control and Prevention 2018), and science education. An example of this type of collaboration is the Clergy Letter Project, a program that encourages faith leaders to affirm support for instruction in evolutionary theory and (more broadly) the compatibility of science and faith (Zimmerman 2018).

Spend Time Together in Person

Perhaps one of the most overlooked and powerful ways to build better understanding between scientists and public communities, including religious communities, is to make actual efforts to spend time together in person. While much has been written on the interface of science and religious faith, and there is much benefit to deep study and discussion of the issues involved, we have found that creating opportunities for people of different life paths and perspectives to spend time together and start what hopefully will be enduring relationships is one of the most likely ways to create real, positive change in people's lives, both for scientists and for those in the public sphere with whom they begin to interact.

CONCLUSION

Echoing points made elsewhere in this book, we believe that science has benefited, and will continue to benefit, society at large. New scientific discoveries and advances can (and should) address looming challenges facing humanity. However, the doing of science and the applications of science and technology are informed by culture, history, and social context. While scientists should be a part of conversations about the role of science in society, their viewpoint will always be among other perspectives in an ecology of decision making. It behooves scientists, science communicators, and teachers to develop skills and strategies for effective engagement with diverse publics, including persons and communities of faith.

REFERENCES

American Association for the Advancement of Science (AAAS). 1990. *Science for all Americans*. New York: Oxford University Press.

American Association for the Advancement of Science (AAAS). 1993. *Benchmarks for science literacy*. New York: Oxford University Press.

American Association for the Advancement of Science (AAAS). 2013. *Atlas of science literacy, Volumes 1 and 2*. Washington, DC: AAAS.

American Association for the Advancement of Science (AAAS). 2015a. Perceptions: Science and religious communities. *www.aaas.org/sites/default/files/content_files/PerceptionsFinalReport.pdf*.

American Association for the Advancement of Science (AAAS). 2015b. Perceptions: Science and religious communities video. *www.aaas.org/page/perceptions-science-and-religious-communities-video*.

American Association for the Advancement of Science (AAAS). 2016. Introducing *Science: The Wide Angle*. *www.scienceforseminaries.org/resources/science-the-wide-angle*.

American Association for the Advancement of Science (AAAS). 2018a. Annual meeting symposia. *www.aaas.org/page/annual-meeting-symposia*.

American Association for the Advancement of Science (AAAS). 2018b. Astronomy engagement with diverse publics. *www.aaas.org/page/astronomy-engagement-diverse-publics*.

American Association for the Advancement of Science (AAAS). 2018c. Dialogue on science, ethics, and religion. *www.aaas.org/DoSER*.

American Association for the Advancement of Science (AAAS). 2018d. DoSER public lectures. *www.aaas.org/page/doser-public-lectures*.

American Association for the Advancement of Science (AAAS). 2018e. DoSER resources. *www.aaas.org/page/doser-resources*.

American Association for the Advancement of Science (AAAS). 2018f. Mission and history. *www. aaas.org/about/mission-and-history.*

American Association for the Advancement of Science (AAAS). 2018g. Resources. *www. scienceforseminaries.org/resources.*

American Association for the Advancement of Science (AAAS). 2018h. Why public engagement matters. *www.aaas.org/pes/what-public-engagement.*

Baker, C., and J. B. Miller. 2006. *The evolution dialogues: Science, Christianity, and the quest for understanding.* Washington, DC: American Association for the Advancement of Science.

Beck, J. 2017. This article won't change your mind. *The Atlantic.* March 13. *www.theatlantic.com/ science/archive/2017/03/this-article-wont-change-your-mind/519093.*

Centers for Disease Control and Prevention. 2018. Preventive health and health services block grant: North Carolina. *www.healthypeople.gov/sites/default/files/Block%20Grant%20North%20 Carolina%20Final%20508-Ready.pdf.*

Ecklund, E. H. 2010. *Science vs. religion: What scientists really think.* New York: Oxford University Press.

Ecklund, E. H., and C. P. Scheitle. 2017. *Religion vs. science: What religious people really think.* New York: Oxford University Press.

Goodall, J. 1990. *Through a window: My thirty years with the chimpanzees of Gombe.* Boston: Houghton Mifflin Harcourt.

Leshner, A. 2017. *The science of science communication III: Inspiring novel collaborations and building capacity.* Arthur M. Sackler Colloquia. *www.youtube.com/watch?v=_ITJ2FUeeKc&t=0s&index= 4&list=PLGJm1x3XQeK2xwsj2vkRgovtvIWSNstex.*

Nisbet, M. 2018. *Scientists in civic life: Facilitating dialogue-based communication.* Washington, DC: AAAS.

Pew Research Center. 2008. U.S. religious landscape survey. *http://assets.pewresearch.org/wp-content/ uploads/sites/11/2008/06/report2-religious-landscape-study-full.pdf.*

Public Agenda. 2014. Same world, different worldviews: How can evangelical Christians and scientists minimize conflict and improve relations? *www.aaas.org/sites/default/files/content_files/ ChoiceworkFinal.pdf.*

Scheller, C. 2017. The Paris agreement & leveraging religious support for climate policy. AAAS. *www.aaas.org/news/paris-agreement-leveraging-religious-support-climate-policy.*

Shetterly, M. L. 2016. *Hidden figures: The American dream and the untold story of the black women who helped win the space race.* New York: William Morrow.

Zimmerman, M. 2018. The clergy letter project. *www.theclergyletterproject.org.*

The Future of Science and Religion in American Schools

David Long

O ver the course of the past 10 or so years, I have been working with college students learning how to teach science. These are our future teachers in training. I teach their methods courses where we take what they have learned in their various university science courses and work with them to think about and become skillful with what moves they will make so that science comes alive for K–12 students. At the same time, I am also a researcher. I am an anthropologist who studies the relationship between science and faith in Americans' lives. It is fascinating work. Schools, including the people within them, are one of the best places to do this research. Schools are not only part of communities, but for some social scientists, they are the site where you can examine how local, regional, and national values are shared. They also, as the story of the American relationship to evolution attests, can be the site of conflict.

SOMETHING MAY BE CHANGING

Regarding some changes that may be afoot in the makeup of American attitudes about science and faith, a recent conversation with a student was telling. In a class I teach for future teachers that explores the history and philosophy of science and math, the subject of religious interpretation and points of conflict came to the fore, as usual. Before the beginning of class, in an adjoining workroom, I often hear students mulling over readings they completed. This evening's class included a segment of Diamond's (1999) *Guns, Germs, and Steel* that is especially good at relating the story of human evolution to the eventual rise of early civilizations. There was a lot of audible mulling. As I entered the class to set up, I could hear one particularly attentive student, Sandy, whose personal artifacts (stickers on a laptop case, summer camp T-shirts, etc.) disclosed her conservative Christian identity, chatting with another about the text. She stated, "My family and I have gone to the Creation Museum a bunch of times. And we have gone to the Ark Experience. But I do not see why people cannot see this [assigned reading] also being true." As Sandy is the kind of student who does not shy away from questions, she turned to me and asked, "Dr. Long, what do you think about this?"

The scene is important for framing our story. I am currently a professor at Morehead State University in the foothills of the Appalachian mountains of Kentucky. While a rural university, it's located in a county known by demographers to be unusual due to some more socially progressive markers such as a large LGBTQ community as well as being a node of Democratic voting patterns amid a sea of strongly Republican counties. At the same time, Rowan County was the site of a sharp tack on the map of U.S. culture wars in recent decades. Kim Davis, the county clerk, had become notable by protesting and eventually going briefly to jail over refusing to sign marriage licenses for same-sex couples. As both the *New York Times* (Blinder and Perez-Pena 2015) and the *Washington Post* (Kaplan and Higdon 2015) reported, communities can indeed work to overcome cultural conflict while remaining deeply split by differences of worldview. Extending this local context to the greater region, as Sandy earlier pointed out, the Answers in Genesis ministries' Creation Museum is a short drive away as is their more recently opened Ark Encounter. The former is the nation's preeminent exhibition of young-Earth creationism and the latter underscores the same message.

As I suggested to Sandy, from my own research with creationist students (Long 2011), most folks are not terribly scientifically literate and that is why I was so glad she was on a path to being a science educator. She is an inquisitive and bright student who listens and cares about science and about other people—a solid foundation for science teaching. But in a turn that crinkled her nose a bit, I also explained that most people are equally or more so religiously illiterate. Many know very strongly that they are members of a religious community, but when you scratch the surface of their religious identity, there often is not very much theological understanding there. When extended past the confines of one's narrow faith tradition, for most, an understanding of other faiths is very limited.

This lack of religious literacy is compounded by how, when encountering new information, many people use what some call cultural cognition or motivated reasoning to accept or reject evidence that confirms or conflicts with what they already know. Motivated reasoning, as we will explore, is a tendency to ignore facts or other cognitively dissonant ideas that your identity finds objectionable. The story those facts tell is not one that your people, whoever they may be, value or celebrate. For a tried-and-true creationist or climate change denier, more evidence supporting evolution and climate change simply gets ignored or artfully rejected. The implications for science teachers should be clear: We do not all reason about evidence in the same way.

As you think about your own family, students, or community members, how much do they know about religious differences at a substantive level? It is most often not very much, as sociologists who study religiosity in the United States have shown (e.g., Wuthnow 2007). Many people know they are faithful, but the content of that faith, for many, is more like being a sports fan of a local team than being a historian or professional commentator on the shapes and contours of the sport.

I have dwelled on setting this research context because, in my experience, it is the *usual* plot for telling the story of science and religion. But as I will point out, demographics are changing rapidly in ways set to potentially shift the conversation about how science and faith interact in American life. Science faces a cultural/cognitive block of motivated reasoning and a changing social landscape, and it is essential for science educators to be prepared for both. For our relationships between science and faith, there are important demographic changes afoot. Americans, on the whole, have quickly begun to self-identify as slightly less religious than prior generations. Of those of faith, almost all of them remain Christians while their denominational identity is changing. Rates of religious belief within racial identities also vary greatly. Each of these factors has great potential to affect relationships between science and religion as we head into the future.

The short story I tell in this closing chapter first examines some highlights needed to foreground the coming demographic changes. Alongside this, I point toward old frameworks for understanding science-and-religion relations that will need to be reconsidered for future social change. Next, I contrast points of tension between evolution and faith groups and how they differ with other areas of science such as climate change. Particularly important to educators, I briefly examine the demographics of the teaching profession and its ability to respond to social changes. Finally, I propose a model for future discourse between people of faith from diverse backgrounds with differing commitments to problems yet to emerge.

A NEW LENS FOR OLD CONFLICT

Many have written about the long, interesting history of how Americans across the breadth and diversity of our experience have related their understanding of science through the lens of their faith. From Numbers's (1998, 2007) histories of how Darwin was initially received and the growth of creationism as a social movement through Laats's (2015) history of conservative social movements (including the 1925 Scopes trial), the United States has been somewhat distinctive in the way its social and religious history related to science. Beyond evolution, newer points of conflict such as disagreement over climate change or vaccine abstention are set to require much more of the public's attention due to their potential for adverse effects. The displacement of coastal populations and the rapid spread of disease due to refusal of our best tools of public health are set to dramatically affect the population in ways that evolution rejection has not.

Changing demographics and a changing understanding of the learning sciences may alter how we see the nature of relations between science and faith and how we need to think about education. While the social history of conflict is well worked through in earlier chapters, a more recent instance orients our conversation toward the future. Some have seen models for dialogue and mutually respected boundaries of questioning and understanding between science and faith, such as Gould's (2002) nonoverlapping magisteria

(NOMA), as useful for quelling conflict. In the NOMA approach, people are expected to play nicely using both science and faith to ask questions and seek answers within distinctly different realms of inquiry. Many professional organizations such as the National Academy of Sciences and Institute of Medicine (2008) have published overview texts such as *Science, Evolution, and Creationism* that essentially take NOMA's lessons to heart.

The audience for such a book, however, often has very little overlap with those most likely to protest the perceived encroachment of science into the social and political aspects of people's work and lives. In short, while NOMA is useful for thinking about differences, the number of people inclined to use those tools remains very, very low. As Gould himself equivocated subtly, NOMA represented a "sound position of general consensus, established by a long struggle among *people of goodwill* [italics added for emphasis] in both magisteria" (Gould 2000). As it happens, there are likely far fewer people of goodwill than what Gould would have hoped for. Understanding how people reason differently through perceived conflict between science and faith requires a mix of insights from sociology, anthropology, and psychology. Evolutionary biology and theology are not enough.

Social science research describing how people actually reason through differences of science and faith has, in the past decade, become a fairly robust area. Depending on your perspective, this phenomenon of human thinking and action is called motivated reasoning or, alternatively, cultural cognition. The basic idea is that people, counter to rational action theory that dominated models of human decision making for decades, are likely to make identity protective moves with their thinking. When faced with information that runs counter to well-entrenched knowledge that supports their stable sense of identity, such individuals dismiss and countervail the information. Douglas's *Natural Symbols* (1974) is perhaps the best early example of models of humans retreating from reasoned evidence in their cultural lives in defense of established, comfortable forms of cognition. This work began the move toward conceptualizing cognition as being filtered through a net that, for most people, is biased toward holding onto existing conceptual schema when they are challenged, rather than being open to new information. In one concrete case, of Americans who have been raised within creationism-supporting church congregations, many students, parents, and sometimes even school administrators and teachers are not open to evidence that forces a reevaluation of parts of their creationist identity. It is likely that, as a reader of this book, you have encountered such people.

Another robust approach to the phenomenon of motivated reasoning stems from the work of psychologists examining "hot and cold" cognition (Sinatra and Pintrich 2003) in the context of understanding evolution rejection. This work, while important and similar in substance to motivated reasoning, was limited due to the focus on individuals rather than the social domain of our mutual cultural existence. This is a crucial point for science educators. As is known from other social science work, we do not reason alone as independent actors. If you are a creationist, you are not committed to such a view willy-nilly. It is a core part of your identity and your membership within a social group that has real ties to community values that bind. Simply changing your identity as an educational project is unlikely to happen easily. The direction of our reasoning is in relation to the myriad things that sustain our identities. We are not purely rational actors. Our reasoning is motivated in many cases to help us remain loyal members of our respective social tribes.

While these points may seem like natural extensions of classical developmental theories of human learning from folks such as Piaget through Vygotsky, they add important new dimensions. When new information puts existing narratives that sustain our identities at risk, we are apt to reject them. In this way, a motivational reasoning model aligns well with others associated with human tribal identities; we often most easily believe what those who share our affinities around us believe. It also explains a lot of why revolutionary advances in the sciences, if they suggest a picture of reality that implies dissonance with religious messaging, are often rejected by many. For example, when Darwinism came to America (Numbers 1998), the type of Christianity being practiced was well primed to find biological evolution troubling (see Chapters 2 and 3 for additional history). For many conservative Christians, this is still the case today.

Through separate strands of sociology, anthropology, psychology, and economics research in recent years, additional trends have emerged. For example, in one telling study, Kahan (2018) shows that, in the case of climate change, most people in the United States show a general low level of scientific literacy. Of those who were most informed, they clearly accepted or rejected the consensus that climate change is happening based almost exclusively on political ideology. Highly educated Democrats tended to accept climate science while highly educated Republicans tended to reject it. What science counts as accurate and useful in interpreting the world, in the case of Kahan's study, depends on your political ideology (see Chapter 5 for additional insight on this). Both Kahan's model of cultural cognition and its similar conceptual cousin, the "backfire effect" (Nyhan and Reifler, 2010), are fruitful starting points to devise more effective science education and science communication strategies going forward.

In my own work with creationists coming to think through the legitimacy of evolution (Long 2011), this research underscores the primacy that students place on local and community values. Tyson, a student with whom I had many conversations, made this very apparent. As he weighed the dissonant messages he was receiving about evolution and climate change, he was clear about the social dimension to his learning and identity:

> It would take a lot of work for me to change my worldview, a lot of time, a lot of alienation from friends. That's a big part of that. I'm always looking and trying to figure out what the Truth is. It's hard. People tend to believe what they've chosen to believe. You believe in something and you'll find a way to believe it. (Long 2011, p. 41)

Tyson's story, in its full form, reads like a script developed to demonstrate the retreat from alienation. He was by no means the only student who felt this way in the course of my research, and perhaps you have had similar students in your classroom.

Expanding from this limited case, the perspective that motivated reasoning brings to science education has additional application in the current political milieu. With the rise of increasingly polarized politics, science educators are at the cutting edge of likely social and cultural pushback from students or other community members. As *New York Times* reporter Amy Harmon detailed in 2017, new teachers are often perplexed regarding how to account for and work with students ready to shut down and turn off from information that contradicts the messages and values of the home. While the growing body of motivated reasoning research has begun to have some effect on the science communication discourse, very little impact to this date has been felt within the science education research community and, by extension, in teacher education and classroom practice. This will need to change, as our ability to engage with global problems such as climate change depends upon it.

SCIENCE, FAITH, AND THE CHANGING DEMOGRAPHY OF THE UNITED STATES

In addition to our growing recognition of motivated reasoning, the shifting religious demography of the United States matters too. For better or worse, conflict between science and faith, with the dominant historical focus being evolution and creationism, has essentially been set in white America. There are plenty of African American and Latino creationists, but their stories have mostly not been told. For myriad reasons, including historically divergent levels of educational attainment, the story about conflict over scientific matters with faith has been a story of and about white Americans.

White and black Americans have more often than not experienced deeply unequal educational experiences. The story told about evolution and creationism—whether via the 1925 Scopes trial, *Epperson's* 1965 challenge to Arkansas law, or the 2005 *Kitzmiller v. Dover Area School District* case in Dover, Pennsylvania—is a story about white people. That does not mean that members of other races were not present in some of the school contexts of these cases. It does mean, however, that the dominant narrative is almost entirely white. The story we know in brief is one of mostly white religious conservatives pushing back against the encroachment of science interests, whether from teachers, professors, or government officials. Where science has been made a character in this story, it has been embodied by white people. This, of course, has not been a complete story of the past and, given pending demographic changes, is one that becomes less salient going forward. The story of science and religion—with changing demography and religious identity no longer numerically dominated by white folks—will have to change.

American demographics have been undergoing a fairly rapid shift in the past few decades. The percentage of all Americans who self-describe as Christian has contracted slightly from 77% percent to 70% in the most recent Pew Religious Landscape Survey (Pew Forum 2009). While this contraction is noteworthy in itself, the category's internal changes are even more notable, especially in the context of examining science and faith. Until recent decades, evangelical and Pentecostal Christians were not considered the dominant or prototypical model of Christian practice. As Borg (1998) has shown and given clear rationale for, Christians who once represented the cultural and demographic core of the faith no longer do so. Mainline Christian congregations (Episcopalian, Methodists, Lutherans, etc.) have been collapsing in number at the expense of growth within evangelical and Pentecostal churches. Evangelical and Pentecostal Christians, whether they one-by-one hold such beliefs actively, are members of denominations that have traditionally had problems with evolution and a handful of other science topics. Whether current and future evangelical groups continue to foster anti-evolution sentiment remains an open question. Certainly there are some evangelical populations that break with dominant trends to have more evolution-friendly positions, but they remain a small minority.

For climate science, there has been hope that a movement of "creation care" (Roberts 2015) would grow appreciably with evangelicals looking to defend the creation from environmental catastrophe. While efforts from evangelical scientists such as Katharine Hayhoe have had some impact, measured against broader national trends, little has changed within this group. One must also remember that the presence of Francis Collins, an evangelical Christian and head of the National Institutes of Health, has had little impact in changing evangelical attitudes about evolution.

Additionally, the number of Americans who self-identify as not religious has grown quickly to levels not seen since polling began. Whereas there have consistently been a few percentage points of atheists and agnostics, a new category of religious *nones* has emerged in the most recent Pew surveys. Whereas most atheists and agnostics have been shown to be among the most scientifically literate of the population, the newer *nones* category does not appear to carry any additional affinity for science. For the nones, religion is just something they neither do nor really think about. What was once a category of largely pro-science Americans is now more complex. Or seen another way, nones may not have a strong opinion about teaching evolution (or not) or including creationism in U.S. schools.

Left out of most conversations on science, faith, and potential conflict are specific breakdowns of attitudes by race. Unlike white Americans of faith, African Americans share a number of demographic markers that make their comparison to white Americans quite distinct. Where evangelicals are more than 75% white in the most recent Pew analysis, mainline Christians are 84% white. As a carryover of the United States' racist history, African American faith communities have been historically almost entirely separated from those of white Americans. Of African Americans, 60% attend historically black Protestant churches, with an additional 15% attending evangelical churches and 5% attending Catholic churches (Pew 2009). African Americans are, by percentage, the most religious of all

American racial groups. Important for understanding science and faith conflicts, historically black Protestant groups share a distinct history from religious conservatives. Most African American Protestant churches practice a theology most concerned with achieving social justice as a reaction to centuries of racial oppression, while simultaneously interpreting scripture in a conservative manner for most other issues. Black American Christianity is unique when measured alongside majority-white American Christian denominations. Whereas majority-white mainline Christian denominations lean more socially liberal and practice a nonliteralist theology, conservative Christians lean socially conservative and tend to practice a literalist theology. In these regards, African American Christians are more like evangelicals in their rejection of evolution.

The Latino experience is varied and complex, as it has been from the founding of the nation to today. Because they are the most rapidly growing ethnic demographic category, Latino relations to science and faith issues will come to matter more and more. By many measures, the relationship between science and faith among the Latino population is similar in overall outlook to white Americans. Latinos are fairly similar to white Americans in attitudes toward evolution (if slightly less inclined to be creationist) and more strongly concerned about the impacts of climate change, with those who speak Spanish being the most concerned about a changing climate (Leiserowitz, Cutler, and Rosenthal 2017).

Interestingly, the longstanding and strong affinity between Latinos and their Catholic identity appears to be changing, with potential impacts for how they relate to science and faith. The fastest-changing demographic indicator of Latino faith practice over the past 20 years is that of declining Catholic identity. Of the two most frequent changes, a bifurcation is seeing one group of Latinos increasingly identifying as evangelical Christians and another joining the growing nones. As U.S. religious practice has historically been fairly racially balkanized, it is difficult to predict whether this shift will have anything to say about the Latino relationship with science.

Changes in demographics that may lead to attitudinal changes regarding science and faith are interesting enough to ponder, but this diversity is not equally distributed across the country. We will also want to project out how science and faith discourses will transfer into schools. As Berkman and Plutzer (2011) found in their representative sample of U.S. biology teachers, the political effects of creationism have been far reaching such that only about 25% of biology teachers teach evolution without downplaying it one way or another. Equally concerning, currently half of U.S. educators make no association between global climate change and its anthropogenic sources (Plutzer et al. 2016).

Confounding these points is the issue of teacher turnover in U.S. schools. The teaching profession has been undergoing a shift from a rapidly aging cohort of baby-boomer teachers to a new cohort who are worryingly short-termed in their professional positions, most staying five years or less. Additionally, the U.S. teacher corps does not look like the

U.S. population. It is far whiter than that of the general population (U.S. Department of Education 2016). If our teacher population comes to look demographically like the country in general—certainly a good thing—it remains an open question whether anti-evolution attitudes that have punctuated some parts of the teaching workforce will substantively change.

TEACHING AND THE FUTURE WE COULD HAVE

While it is not usually the first thing that we focus on as science educators in our communication with students, colleagues, or community members, the act of teaching is underpinned by a belief in, and hope for, a better future. While we do not necessarily share the same identity and ideology across populations, as this brief chapter has shown, we as educators invest our time and energy in the work we do as idealists, and we truly believe that growing understanding can foster a better and more interesting future.

We can and should use the tools we already have, and that have been outlined in this book, to create learning environments in our classrooms that expand students' understanding of all scientific phenomena, regardless of what implications such knowledge has for specific worldviews and identities. This requires the preparation of teachers in colleges and the ongoing commitment to a certain politics of teaching, including one that respects religious identity while encouraging the full flourishing of scientific understanding in our students. Right now, in the case of evolution education, we have far too many teachers across the nation eliminating or downplaying evolution in their classrooms in deference to local religious values (Berkman and Plutzer 2011; Long 2011). By doing so, such teachers may quell local conflict, but they ultimately fail the educational mission of science.

"While we do not necessarily share the same identity and ideology across populations, we as educators invest our time and energy in the work we do as idealists, and we truly believe that growing understanding can foster a better and more interesting future."

We also insist on a separation of church and state when it comes to science education, not in a hostile, confining way but rather in deference to the flourishing of all views, including the grand narrative of science, in a way where each is practiced in its appropriate domain. We can refer to religious views to understand why some people object to science, but we cannot defer to religious views in service of a better understanding of science. Efforts such as those of the Discovery Institute detailed earlier in this book (Chapters 2 and 3 in particular) have shown their first mission to be evangelism, not science. While imperfect, we have good models for effective science education discourse that lay out the general rules of the communication game. Science teachers can preempt potential conflict by a good faith effort at bringing all students under a collective agreement to play by such rules.

One approach that I recommend is called ideal speech, and it is similar to the practical suggestions presented in Part II of this book. This is a philosophical model in which all ideas can be expressed by competent people playing by a certain set of productive, critical discourse rules (Habermas 1984). As this chapter and the idea of motivated reasoning have pointed toward, this will be very hard work requiring new ways of thinking about science teaching. When facing challenges such as how to improve public receptivity to climate change, we have no other choice. We have structured the educational experience for American children such that the school is the first, and sometimes only, place where people with dramatically different worldviews come together to collectively deliberate about the natural world. We as educators need to be good at our charge.

The road ahead for science and faith in education may be primed for ongoing or increasing conflict. Despite this priming, hopefully newer generations of Americans, with the help of well-equipped science teachers, can find both the mutual respect needed for scientific understanding as well as an underscoring of our nation's founding commitment to respect for all religious faiths. As this book has shown, in our diverse nation with people of myriad faiths, we need this commitment to tolerance and scientific growth to direct what we ought to be doing. Science and technology can be wielded in any direction, toward ends both fruitful and terrible for human life. As educators, we have a special charge to balance our interests across science and faith, ensuring that we move willfully toward a more just future that's filled with opportunities for all to flourish regardless of the domain of understanding from which that comes.

REFERENCES

Berkman, M. B., and E. Plutzer. 2011. Defeating creationism in the courtroom, but not in the classroom. *Science* 331 (6016): 404–405.

Blinder, A., and R. Perez-Pena. *New York Times.* 2015. Kentucky clerk denies same-sex marriage licenses, defying court. September 1.

Borg, M. J. 1998. *The God we never knew: Beyond dogmatic religion to a more authentic contemporary faith.* New York: Harper Collins.

Diamond, J. 1999. *Guns, germs, and steel: The fates of human societies.* New York: Norton.

Douglas, M. 1974. *Natural symbols: Explorations in cosmology.* New York: Random House.

Gould, S. J. 2000. Evolution and the 21st century. Paper presented at the Annual Meeting of the American Institute of Biological Sciences, Washington, DC.

Gould, S. J. 2002. *Rocks of ages: Science and religion in the fullness of life.* New York: Ballantine.

Habermas, J. 1984. *Theory of communicative action.* Trans. Thomas A. McCarthy. Boston: Beacon Press.

Harmon, A. *New York Times.* 2017. Climate science meets a stubborn obstacle: Students. June 4.

Kahan, D. 2018. The cultural cognition project. *www.culturalcognition.net.*

Kahneman, D. 2013. *Thinking, fast and slow.* New York: Farrar, Straus and Giroux.

Kaplan, S., and J. Higdon. *Washington Post.* 2015. The defiant Kim Davis, the Ky. clerk who refuses to issue gay marriage licenses. September 1.

Laats, A. 2015. *The other school reformers: Conservative activism in American education.* Cambridge, MA: Harvard University Press.

Leiserowitz, A., M. Cutler, and S. Rosenthal. 2017. Climate change on the Latino mind. *http:// climatecommunication.yale.edu/publications/climate-change-latino-mind-may-2017.*

Long, D. E. 2011. *Evolution and religion in American education: An ethnography.* Dordrecht, Netherlands: Springer.

National Academy of Sciences and Institute of Medicine. 2008. *Science, evolution, and creationism.* Washington, DC: National Academies Press.

Numbers, R. L. 1998. *Darwinism comes to America.* Cambridge, MA: Harvard University Press.

Numbers, R. L., and International Society for Science and Religion. 2007. *The creationists: From scientific creationism to intelligent design.* Cambridge, MA: International Society for Science and Religion.

Nyhan, B., and J. Reifler. 2010. When corrections fail: The persistence of political misperceptions. *Political Behavior* 32 (2): 303–330.

Pew Forum on Religion & Public Life. 2009. *U.S. religious landscape survey.* Washington, DC: Pew Forum on Religion & Public Life.

Plutzer, E., M. McCaffrey, A. L. Hannah, J. Rosenau, M. Berbeco, and A. H. Reid. 2016. Climate confusion among U.S. teachers. *Science* 351 (6274): 664–665.

Roberts, D. 2015. Creation Care tried to bring evangelicals into the climate movement. Here's why it failed. *www.vox.com/2015/11/13/9729884/creation-care-evangelicals-climate-change.*

Sinatra, G. M., and P. R. Pintrich. 2003. *Intentional conceptual change.* Mahwah, NJ: L. Erlbaum.

U.S. Department of Education. 2016. *The state of racial diversity in the educator workforce.* Washington, DC: U.S. Department of Education, Office of Planning, Evaluation and Policy Development, Policy and Program Studies Service.

Wuthnow, R. 2007. *America and the challenges of religious diversity.* Princeton, NJ: Princeton University Press.

Index